THE ART OF

STAR WARS

GALAXY

VOLUME TWO

THE ART OF

VOLUME TWO

Written & Edited
By Gary Gerani

Designed By
Michaelis / Carpelis design

TOPPS PUBLISHING • NEW YORK

Preceding spread: Illustrator Walter Simonson's chase card art for Star Wars Galaxy Two. Color by Arthur Suydam. Chase cards from the first and second series fit together to form a larger scene. Right: Simonson's preliminary sketches.

THE ART OF STAR WARS GALAXY: VOLUME TWO IS PUBLISHED BY TOPPS PUBLISHING, ONE WHITEHALL STREET, NEW YORK, NY 10004. TM & © 1994 LUCASFILM LTD. ALL RIGHTS RESERVED. USED UNDER AUTHORIZATION. THIS BOOK MAY NOT BE REPRODUCED IN ANY FORM, WITHOUT WRITTEN PERMISSION OF THE PUBLISHER.

PRINTED IN CANADA
FIRST EDITION: NOVEMBER, 1994

COVER PAINTING BY BORIS VALLEJO

10 9 8 7 6 5 4 3 2 1

LIBRARY OF CONGRESS CATALOGING-IN-PUBLICATION DATA

ISBN 1-883313-03-1

94-61049
CIP

DISTRIBUTION TO BOOKSTORES IS PROVIDED BY THE BERKLEY PUBLISHING GROUP.

COMPANIES, PROFESSIONAL GROUPS, CLUBS, AND OTHER ORGANIZATIONS MAY QUALIFY FOR SPECIAL TERMS WHEN ORDERING QUANTITIES OF THIS TITLE. FOR INFORMATION WRITE: SPECIAL SALES, TOPPS PUBLISHING, ONE WHITEHALL STREET, NEW YORK, NY 10004 OR CALL: 212/376-0478.

A LIMITED AMOUNT OF COPIES OF *The Art of Star Wars Galaxy: Volume One* ARE AVAILABLE AND MAY BE PURCHASED BY MAIL. SEND $23.00, POSTPAID, CHECK OR MONEY ORDER TO: TOPPS/GALAXY VOLUME ONE, P.O. BOX 48, DURYEA, PA 18642. OFFER GOOD IN U.S. AND CANADA ONLY. WHILE SUPPLIES LAST.

SPECIAL THANKS TO OUR COLLEAGUES AT LUCASFILM LICENSING FOR THEIR EXTRAORDINARY SUPPORT AND ASSISTANCE: HOWARD ROFFMAN, JULIA RUSSO, GARY HYMOWITZ, ALLAN KAUSCH, SUE ROSTONI, STACY MOLLEMA AND KATHLEEN SCANLON. WE ARE ESPECIALLY GRATEFUL TO LUCY AUTREY WILSON, LUCASFILM DIRECTOR OF PUBLISHING, FOR HER ENTHUSIASM AND GUIDANCE.

ADDITIONAL SPECIAL THANKS TO ILLUSTRATOR RALPH MCQUARRIE WHOSE BREATHTAKING ART AND RECOLLECTIONS ADDED IMMEASURABLY TO THE PROJECT.

MANY OTHER DEDICATED PEOPLE AND COMPANIES PLAYED AN IMPORTANT PART IN THE CREATION OF THIS BOOK. FROM THE DESIGN BY MICHAELIS/CARPELIS DESIGN INC. TO THE SEPARATIONS BY COLOR SYSTEMS AND THE PRINTING BY QUEBECOR, WE APPRECIATE THE TENDER LOVING CARE TAKEN BY THESE FIRMS AND THEIR TALENTED STAFFS. FROM TOPPS, INGAR WESTBURG AND JOHN WILLIAMS KEPT THE BALL ROLLING, CLAUDIA CANNY HANDLED THE DATA ENTRY AND MARK WEINTRAUB COORDINATED THE OVERALL PRODUCTION. STEPHEN J. SANSWEET'S INVALUABLE CONTRIBUTION TO OUR GALAXY CARD SET FIGURED IMPORTANTLY IN THIS BOOK, AS WAS OUR ACCESS TO THE ORIGINAL ART COLLECTION OF BILL PLUMB AND EXTENSIVE COMIC RESEARCH BY JEFFERY LINDENBLATT. LAST, AND CERTAINLY NOT LEAST, WE TIP OUR HATS TO ALL THE WONDERFULLY TALENTED ARTISTS WHOSE WORK APPEARS ON THESE PAGES. WITHOUT THEIR CREATIVE VISION AND OUTSTANDING ABILITY, WE WOULD NOT HAVE HAD THE PRIVILEGE OF PUBLISHING THIS BOOK.

QUOTES USED IN *The Art of Star Wars Galaxy: Volume Two* WERE DERIVED FROM VIDEO DOCUMENTARIES, MOVIE MAGAZINES AND PERSONAL INTERVIEWS. (NOTE: PAGE NUMBERS REFER TO PAGES IN *THIS* BOOK).

Star Wars Trilogy: The Definitive Collection—LASERDISC SUPPLEMENT. (1993, FOX VIDEO) PAGES 18, 32, 33, 34, 52, 72, 74, 85, 86, 101
Cinefantastique Star Wars DOUBLE-ISSUE VOL. 6 NO. 4, VOL. 7 NO. 1 (1978, FREDRICK S. CLARKE) PAGES 18, 21, 22, 74, 84, 100
Fantastic Films VOL. 4, NO. 1 (1981) PAGES 51, 112

Contents

FOREWORD

As an illustrator and concept design-er, working on the *Star Wars* movies was the most fun I've ever had. George Lucas' galaxy of fantastic planets, life forms and technology certainly pre-sented a daunting challenge. Nothing like it had ever been attempted on the motion picture screen before. As things turned out, *Star Wars* and every-one's response to it exceeded our own expectations. The public readily accepted Wookiees and Jawas, Death Stars and X-wing fighters...all compo-nents of a gritty, used, decidedly "real" universe. The fact that this universe continues to enthrall and inspire view-ers so many years after its first appear-ance is a testament to George Lucas' fertile imagination.

Projects like Topps' STAR WARS GALAXY cards and the upcoming book, *The Illustrated Star Wars Universe*, enable us to fill in some of the exciting details that have been in the back of our minds since the first three films were produced. We can re-visit the planets and alien cultures introduced in the Saga and use our creative imagina-tions to explore them more fully.

All in all, projects such as these form a bridge between George's origi-nal, groundbreaking creations, and the wondrous adventures soon to come. Playing an important role in the real-ization of these adventures—past, pre-sent and future—is a source of enor-mous pride for me.

Thank you, George.

Ralph McQuarrie

INTRODUCTION

It was the ultimate tough act to follow, but George Lucas and his collaborators had the Force as their ally. *The Empire Strikes Back* enthralled 1980 audiences by expanding and enhancing concepts introduced in *Star Wars*, while retaining the spirited sense of wonder that made the first movie such a classic.

As the second series of STAR WARS GALAXY trading cards began taking

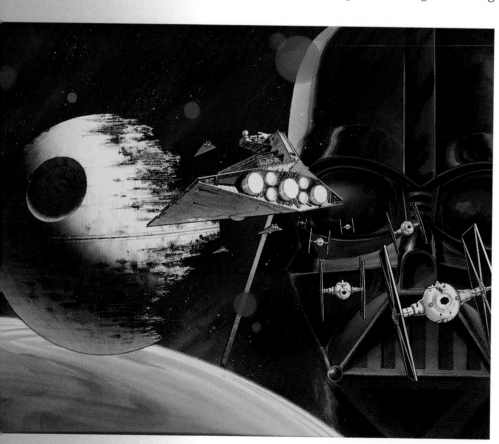

shape, we at Topps faced a similar challenge. The first GALAXY set (1993) had been enormously successful; it was widely hailed as a breakthrough in non-sports trading cards. Like *Empire*, our 135-card sequel required a powerful identity of its own. The goal was to deliver the same kind of excitement—only differently—enlarging the scope of our editorial content while confidently blasting off into new directions of style.

With one important exception, the

*VARIOUS VIEWS OF THE STAR WARS COS-
MOS. OPPOSITE PAGE, TOP: AN UNUSED
JEDI POSTER CONCEPT PAINTED BY
KAZUHIKO SANO. BOTTOM: A LUNCH BOX
ILLUSTRATION BY EAST COAST ADVERTISING
ARTIST GENE LEMERY. THIS PAGE, LEFT:
GEORGE GAADT'S FANCIFUL PORTRAIT OF
LUCAS AND FRIENDS, USED IN A 1982
READER'S DIGEST ARTICLE. BELOW: A PAIR
OF POSTER CONCEPT PRELIMS BY KAZUHIKO
SANO (TOP) AND JOHN SOLIL (BOTTOM).*

creative team of this second series
pretty much mirrored the first. I was,
again, back at the helm as Editor-in-
Chief, structuring the contents, making
selections and pulling all of the
diverse sub-categories together.
Consulting Editor Steve Sansweet
returned with amazing visuals and
invaluable information. Topps' Ingar
Westburg assumed the role of
Managing Editor of GALAXY TWO,
working closely with "New Visions"
artists while tracking the product's
design with assistant John Williams
(*not* the composer). Other Toppers
hovering about helpfully were Ira
Friedman (Vice President, Publishing),
Greg Goldstein (Director of
Publishing), Jim Salicrup (Editor-in-
Chief, Topps Comics), Len Brown
(Creative Director), Don Alan
Zakrzewski (Design Director) and Mark
Weintraub (Production Coordinator).

As the card set evolved, it began to

A pen-and-ink "New Visions" portrait of Lando Calrissian, rendered with a Flash Gordon-like flourish by Rich Buckler. Below, Buckler's pencil prelim. Way below: one of President Reagan's SDI fever dreams depicted in a classic political cartoon by Pulitzer Prize winning Tony Auth.

resemble *The Empire Strikes Back* in ways we hadn't anticipated. The colors white and blue dominated a good deal of our artwork, subtly suggesting *Empire*'s "cool" look (by comparison, GALAXY ONE radiates Tatooine-like orange and amber). Early on in the selection of imagery, Steve Sansweet recommended we include a dramatic,

A lively Kenner collage by the Cato Yasumura Behaeghel Studio. Lower left: A rough poster concept for Return of The Jedi (artist unknown). Circle: Morgan Weistling's breathtaking collector's plate for The Empire Strikes Back.

when revealed in *The Empire Strikes Back.*

To achieve our "better the second time around" goals of surprise and diversity, entirely new sub-sets were conceived. Ralph McQuarrie's creative contributions were paid homage in a section that boasted four never-before-published paintings rendered by McQuarrie for an upcoming Bantam book, *The Illustrated Star Wars Universe.* Since the *Star Wars* saga enjoyed a rich history in the comic book medium, an elaborate sub-set exploring everything from Marvel's earliest adaptations to Dark Horse's cur-

face-to-face study of Darth and Luke by illustrator Don Punchatz. Eventually chosen for our title card, this painting set the tone for the entire series; capturing the essence of the father-son conflict that resonated so sharply

TWO RARE, UNSIGNED CONCEPT PAINTINGS COMMISSIONED FOR THE EMPIRE STRIKES BACK. THESE AND OTHER UNPUBLISHED ILLUSTRATIONS WERE RECENTLY DISCOVERED AT THE LUCASFILM ARCHIVES.

rent achievements was also in order. Art collector William Plumb generously opened up his archives and provided a plethora of memorable illustrations. From Alec Guinness' self-portrait as Obi-Wan to the Ronald Reagan caricatures in political cartoons by Tony Auth, it was an eclectic, attention-grabbing group that added a different dimension to the series.

Of course, original production and promotion art continues to intrigue most *Star Wars* enthusiasts. For GALAXY TWO, Steve Sansweet returned from the Lucasfilm Archives

with all manner of poster and character designs; the majority of which had never been seen, let alone printed, before. Finally, the number of our New Visions commissions was increased and some truly remarkable pieces were crafted. Among these works was the last original rendering by the late Jack Kirby, comicdom's most celebrated innovator.

To top off the project, fantasy specialist Boris Vallejo was approached to paint the signature "key art," an unusually active, character-rich portrait of the droids under attack.

TOP: BEN KENOBI AS RENDERED BY SIR ALEC GUINNESS. LEFT: A MAGNIFICENT "NEW VISIONS" PORTRAIT OF THE YOUNG OBI-WAN BY AUSTRALIAN ILLUSTRATOR HUGH FLEMING. BOTTOM: KENOBI'S FORMER PUPIL, THE DREADED DARTH VADER SCULPTED BY TODD ANDREWS FOR A SERIES OF PEWTER STATUETTES.

In the final analysis, we hope that this ambitious combination of creative elements known as STAR WARS GALAXY TWO is a sequel worthy of its inspiration. Whether we card creators have succeeded in equaling or even topping ourselves is something you can decide after the exhibition is over.

In the meantime, sit back, rev up your imaginations and prepare to be rocketed into the universe according to George Lucas...the once and future STAR WARS GALAXY.

Gary Gerani, 1994

Top: Markus' pinball game art, printed on a plastic sheet for Data East. Right: Scott Gustafson's whimsical 1981 cover painting for Fantastic Films magazine. Opposite page: the climactic Jedi space battle, illustrated by Michael David Ward for a Lucasfilm Fan Club magazine cover.

CHAPTER ONE

THE McQUARRIE PORTFOLIO

"I never really thought *Star Wars* would become a film when I was working on those original paintings," admits concept designer Ralph McQuarrie. "It seemed so funky at the time, so vast a project..."

As all movie historians know, it was McQuarrie's dazzling preproduction vistas that helped sell *Star Wars* to Twentieth Century-Fox in the first place. Right after the success of *American Graffiti*, George Lucas and producer Gary Kurtz visited the illustrator and commissioned him to develop a series of imaginative paintings and sketches. These showcased the landscapes, costumes and vehicles for their proposed, untitled science-fantasy extravaganza. "It seemed to (Lucas) a good idea to have some illustrations to show the scope of the visuals that he'd planned, which in George's mind was a big part of the movie." Today, it's commonplace for a comic book or video game to be adapted into a multi-million dollar motion picture. But back in the mid-70's, this type of high-powered fantasia was virtually unheard of. No wonder *Star Wars* was perceived as "funky."

Reflecting on that fateful commission, Ralph McQuarrie has no problems being known today as "the *Star*

RALPH MCQUARRIE WORKS MOSTLY IN ACRYLICS AND GOUACHE, SOMETIMES USING COLORED PENCILS AND AIRBRUSH. OPPOSITE PAGE: NEWLY-CONCEIVED ART DEPICTING A BATTLE BETWEEN RIVAL SWAMP DENIZENS ON DAGOBAH. THIS PAGE, LEFT: ANOTHER SLIMY RESIDENT OF THE SWAMP PLANET, A MONSTER SPIDER. TOP: LUKE CONFRONTS DARTH VADER IN THE CARBON-FREEZING CHAMBER ON BESPIN.

Wars artist." Over the years he's worked on both of the film's sequels, various television spin-offs and all kinds of unusual tie-ins, ranging from Yoda Christmas cards to a nifty "We're moving!" illustration distributed by Lucasfilm when the company left Universal City. Just recently, McQuarrie completed work on a new Bantam book entitled *The Illustrated Star Wars Universe.* "It's kind of like a National Geographic approach to this material," the artist explains. "We'll be visiting planets and cultures just hinted at in the original films."

Since the second series of *Star Wars Galaxy* was in development at the same time as McQuarrie's book, and since we were planning a special subset on the illustrator, it was inevitable

McQuarrie's unpublished, awe-inspiring realization of the entertainment center on Coruscant, the galactic seat of government. Inset: An interesting concept of two Death Stars being built simultaneously. In an earlier phase of the artist's career, he painted rockets for CBS News and their animated Apollo flight projects. "That's probably what got me interested in movies," McQuarrie recollects.

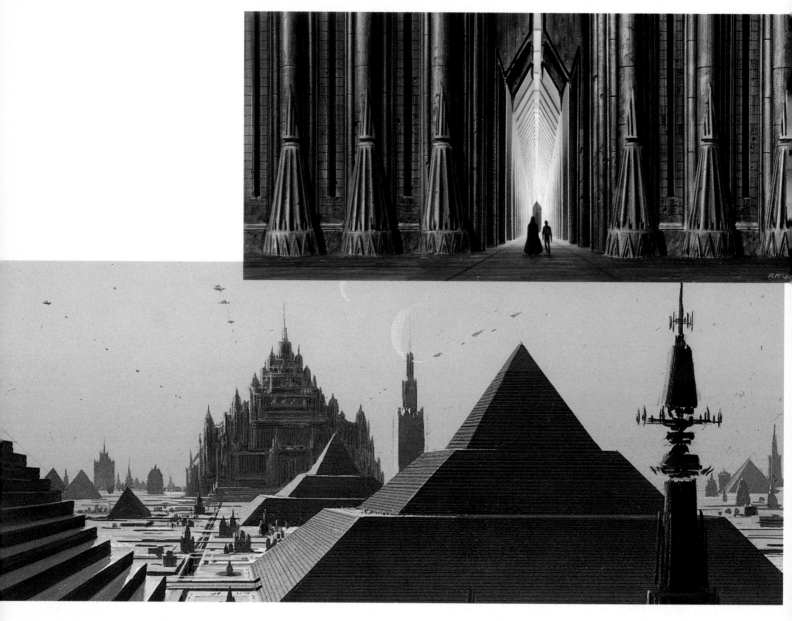

TOP: LORD VADER AND A COMPANION ENTER THE CATHEDRAL-LIKE IMPERIAL PALACE OF CORUSCANT. ABOVE: A VIEW OF THE IMPERIAL CITY, SPECTACULARLY FILLED WITH PYRAMID-LIKE BUILDINGS AND OTHER EXOTIC STRUCTURES.

these projects would overlap. Consequently, we were ecstatic when four of McQuarrie's newly-conceived paintings were made available to us for an exclusive preview.

Born in Gary, Indiana, the 65 year old artist grew up in Montana and spent the first twenty years of his professional career as a commercial artist, doing work mostly for the aerospace industry. "I was always interested in

military aircraft and rockets. I was kind of engineering oriented," McQuarrie notes, although movies and eventually movie-related assignments would lure him into the Hollywood mainstream. Ultimately, it was George Lucas' off-beat brainchild that united these creative interests and enabled the remarkable designer to focus and fine-tune his considerable talents.

"My inspiration comes to me like

bubbles rising in a champagne bottle," he observed in a 1977 interview. "I lay down and rest. The ideas come from somewhere inside me and rise slowly to the conscious level. Then I awake and paint my pictures."

Judging from his recent accomplishments, the Force of pure imagination is still very much with Ralph McQuarrie. His distinctive sensibility which helped shape the most important science fantasy movies of all time, will undoubtedly continue to amaze and excite us in the years to come.

Two never-before-seen McQuarrie visions. Left: Giant platforms float high over Bespin mining Tibanna gas. Below: The frozen geysers of Hoth are trampled by a trio of Imperial walkers.

CHAPTER TWO

COMIC ART

Unlike great comic books that have inspired successful movies, *Star Wars* was a great movie that inspired successful comic book projects. These were published by two leading companies at two different stages of the Saga's history. Originally the property was Marvel's 1977 jewel in the crown, blasting into orbit with Roy Thomas at the controls as both writer and editor. It was an enthusiastic Thomas, personally selected by comics fan and reader George Lucas, who "sold" Marvel on *Star Wars* to begin

MARVEL ARTISTS STRUT THEIR STUFF IN A SERIES OF MEMORABLE PIN-UPS. *OPPOSITE PAGE, COUNTER-CLOCKWISE*: JOE JUSKO, JOHN BYRNE, MARSHALL ROGERS. *THIS PAGE, LEFT*: FRANK MILLER, BOB LAYTON. *BELOW*: DAVE DORMAN'S LUSH COVER PAINTING OF "ANOTHER HUTT" IN *TALES OF THE JEDI* (DARK HORSE). DORMAN HAS BEEN ILLUSTRATING COVERS, MOST OF A FANTASTIC NATURE, FOR OVER FIFTEEN YEARS.

with. As should have been obvious, Lucas' imaginative material was ideally suited to the colorful, hyperkinetic, flashily fantastic medium of comics. Once the movie appeared, the Howard Chaykin-illustrated adaptations became smash hits, insuring *Star Wars* a long and profitable run with the company (until 1986, two blockbuster sequels later).

The Marvel years produced some memorable interpretations by both veteran illustrators like Carmine Infantino and young hotshots like Arthur Adams and Walter Simonson. In addition to the ongoing narrative (Archie Goodwin took over Thomas' writing/editorial duties after awhile), Marvel presented a number of impres-

sive, poster-like comic illustrations inside each book. These pin-ups—rendered by industry superstars—formed a remarkable portfolio apart from the main comics feature and were fondly remembered.

When it came time to develop GALAXY TWO's Comics History subset, Topps resurrected the classic pin-ups as trading cards, with all new, state-of-the-art color provided by Digital Chameleon. Thanks to their frequently miraculous service these illustrations achieved a new brilliance.

While the original *Star Wars* comic books were enjoying a robust run, *Star Wars* comic *strips* designed for newspaper syndication were also very much in demand. This provided fertile creative ground for the seasoned team of Marvel's Archie Goodwin and comics legend Al Williamson. Williamson proved the ultimate choice to illustrate Lucas' far-away worlds, concepts and characters. Apart from his EC Comics sci-fi background, the Alex Raymond-inspired artist had illustrated a wondrous *Flash Gordon* newspaper strip for King Features and specialized in classical, swashbuckling heroes and villains. It's fair to say Williamson found the "Stewart Granger" in Han

Solo, and dream-cities like Bespin never looked more beautiful or elegant. He also found time to render two equally impressive, full-length comics adaptations of E*mpire* and J*edi*.

In recent years, the comic book destiny of *Star Wars* has been in the capable hands of publisher Mike Richardson's Dark Horse Comics, a company that wasn't even in existence when the original *Star Wars* comics

OPPOSITE PAGE: MICHAEL GOLDEN'S EXPLOSIVE "CHICKEN" WALKER ATTACK ON HOTH, A MARVEL COMICS PIN-UP. ABOVE DAVE DORMAN ILLUSTRATES "ULIC QEL-DROMA AND THE BEAST WARS OF ONDERON," A TALES OF THE JEDI STORY BY TOM VEITCH (DARK HORSE).

were running. Promoted to heavy-hitter status in the industry with comic adaptations of *Predator*, *Alien* and *Terminator*, Dark Horse also creates its own comic characters (such as *The Mask*) and oft-times re-invents movie properties in the form of extremely well-conceived and executed graphic novels.

Certainly among the best of these was *Dark Empire* (1991), a critically-acclaimed sequel to the Saga written by Tom Veitch with magnificent interior artwork by Cam Kennedy. This series told the dramatic tale of how Luke Skywalker became seduced by the dark side of the Force, only to be

DAVE DORMAN COVER ARTWORK FOR THE DARK EMPIRE SERIES PUBLISHED BY DARK HORSE. "I TRIED TO ACHIEVE A MOVIE POSTER-LIKE FEEL, AS WELL AS TELL A STORY," THE ARTIST SAYS. BELOW: AL WILLIAMSON'S ELEGANT LINE WAS PERFECTLY SUITED TO THE EMPIRE STRIKES BACK AND OTHER STAR WARS COMICS ASSIGNMENTS FOR MARVEL.

TERRY AUSTIN CELEBRATES THE REBELS OF HOTH IN A CLASSIC MARVEL PIN-UP. UPPER RIGHT: A JOHN B. HIGGINS PAINTED COVER FOR MARVEL'S BRITISH EDITION OF THE EMPIRE STRIKES BACK.

pulled back into the light by his sister, Leia, whose own Jedi powers blossomed at story's end. Cover illustrator Dave Dorman provided a series of luminous character studies that, as the artist puts it, "pretty much tell the entire story right up front. We dealt with a lot of montage imagery, partially because we wanted to capture a

movie poster-like approach, but mainly because it seemed like the most effective way to portray the inner conflicts of the characters."

Hot on the best-selling heels of *Dark Empire* was Dark Horse's follow-up series, *Tales of the Jedi* (1993). Also written by Tom Veitch, this was a Lucasfilm-sanctioned attempt to expand the scope and history of the *Star Wars* universe by introducing major new events and characters.

"I approached the covers for *Tales of the Jedi* with a very different attitude," offers Dave Dorman. "There was much more freedom on that project. To begin with, we didn't have to worry about likeness approval, since none of

the original characters were involved. Also, because the stories took place thousands of years before *Dark Empire*, the level of technology was relatively primitive and civilization was more barbaric. So for these covers I tried to be a little looser, a bit more primal and dramatic with large, simple images."

Judging from what's in development (*Dark Empire: The Second Series* and *Dark Lords of the Sith* from Dark Horse, more GALAXY trading cards and magazines from Topps), it appears *Star Wars* will be flourishing in the comics medium for a good many years to come.

LEFT: LEIA IS CERTAINLY GOING TO HAVE HER HANDS FULL PULLING THE DARK-SIDED LUKE BACK INTO THE LIGHT. ANOTHER STRIKING COVER PAINTING FROM DARK EMPIRE BY DAVE DORMAN. ABOVE: TWO MAJESTIC DARK EMPIRE INTERIOR PANELS BY CAM KENNEDY.

CHAPTER THREE

LIKE FATHER, LIKE SON?

It was the most chilling line of dialogue in the entire *Star Wars* trilogy: "I am your father!" Darth Vader tells a stunned Luke Skywalker at the climax of *The Empire Strikes Back*.

Luke wasn't the only one who was stunned. Filmgoers who reveled in the first movie's high-spirited whimsy and *Wizard of Oz*-like sense of benign adventure were now plunged down darker, bleaker corridors. Likable characters evolved, losing some of their innocence, and disturbing new dimensions emerged. Then that unforgettable, exquisitely nasty plot twist...Suddenly the *Star Wars* saga meant more than just an abstract battle of Good vs. Evil, spectacular dogfights and semi-satiric, monster-populated set pieces.

"The original concept really related to a father and a son and twins," George Lucas confirmed in an overview of the three films. "It was that relationship that was the core of the story."

Arriving at that story, however, was a long and curious process; in many

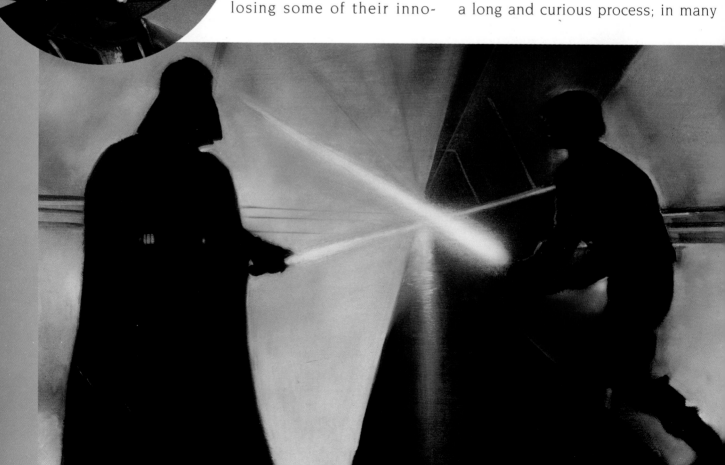

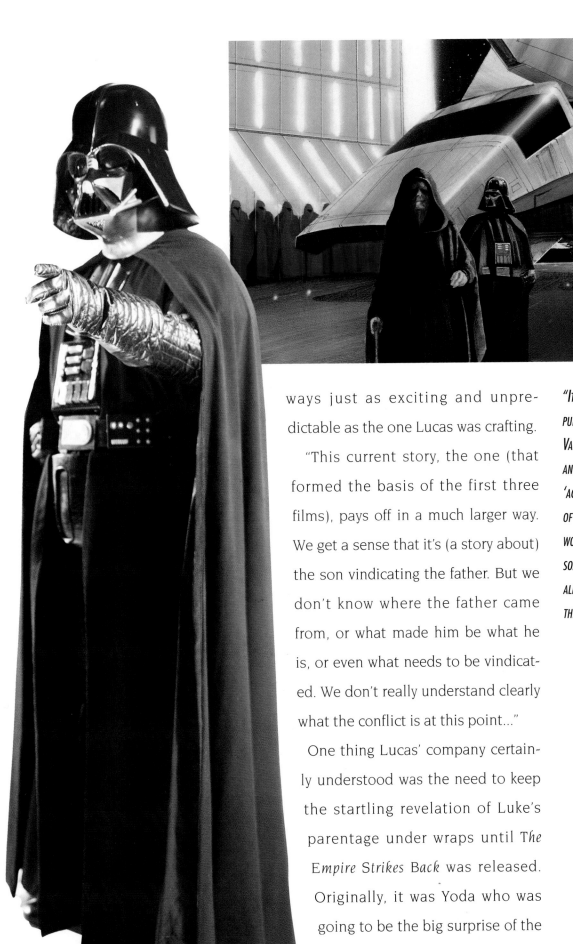

ways just as exciting and unpredictable as the one Lucas was crafting.

"This current story, the one (that
formed the basis of the first three
films), pays off in a much larger way.
We get a sense that it's (a story about)
the son vindicating the father. But we
don't know where the father came
from, or what made him be what he
is, or even what needs to be vindicat-
ed. We don't really understand clearly
what the conflict is at this point..."

One thing Lucas' company certainly understood was the need to keep
the startling revelation of Luke's
parentage under wraps until *The
Empire Strikes Back* was released.
Originally, it was Yoda who was
going to be the big surprise of the
movie. Images of the little Jedi

*"IT REALLY TAKES A TOP-CLASS ACTOR TO
PULL OFF (THE SPEAKING ROLE OF DARTH
VADER)," OBSERVES GEORGE LUCAS. "IN
ANIMATION, AT LEAST, YOU GET TO SORT OF
'ACT IT' AND CREATE IT. BUT IN THE CASE
OF VADER, JAMES EARL JONES HAD TO
WORK WITHIN THE CONFINES OF WHAT
SOMEBODY ELSE (DAVID PROWSE) HAD
ALREADY CREATED...THE MOVEMENT AND
THE TIMING AND THAT SORT OF THING."*

DARTH VADER (DAVID PROWSE) SHARES THE FRAME WITH BOTH GRAND MOFF TARKIN (PETER CUSHING) ON THE ORIGINAL DEATH STAR AND SON LUKE SKYWALKER (MARK HAMILL) IN THE EMPEROR'S THRONE ROOM.

master were going to be withheld from both publicity and the various licensees connected to *Empire*. Realizing there was no feasible way to keep Yoda invisible (how was Marvel going to produce a comic book adaptation without showing him?), Lucasfilm relented. But information about Luke and Darth's biological connection was absent from the screenplay we licensees read when we were preparing our respective projects—which is why there is no mention of it in the original *Empire* trading card series I wrote and edited back in 1980.

Of course, the concept itself is a byproduct of George Lucas' interest in classic mythology and the works of philosopher Joseph Campbell. Campbell's celebrated writings, with their focus on history and sociology, inspired and greatly influenced the young filmmaker.

"I tried to distill down into certain basic ideas things that seemed to exist in a great deal of mythology," Lucas explains, "themes and ideas that continue over a great amount of time and across a wide spectrum of cultures."

Of the great mythical concepts Lucas developed for the *Star Wars* saga, the transmission of power—both good and evil—from father to son remains the most dramatic. It plays off an equally strong classical notion; that of a son avenging the violent, premature death of his father by embarking on a heroic crusade against evil.

"What Luke is doing in the beginning of *Star Wars* is finding his own responsibility for his place in the world," Lucas clarifies. "He thinks that his responsibility is with his aunt and uncle, doing his chores - but his ultimate responsibility is much larger than that because it deals with a much larger base of humanity… larger and more cosmic issues…"

The fact that Luke has to risk not only his life but the fate of the entire galaxy in order to save his father's soul pretty much epitomizes those "larger cosmic issues" our young hero must confront.

In the end, this tale of two Skywalkers became a full-fledged family affair, with Princess Leia the latest member. Like Father, Like Son, Like Daughter? As Vader once put it, "the circle is now complete." Where it leads is something we can discover in comic book sequels like *Dark Empire*, in new novels like *Heir to the Empire*, or perhaps in future *Star Wars* film trilogies produced by George Lucas.

FROM ONE GENERATION TO THE NEXT, A JEDI KNIGHT PASSES ON HIS POWERS…BUT WILL THE DARK SIDE OF THE FORCE PREVAIL? THE HEART AND SOUL OF THE STAR WARS TRILOGY, CAPTURED BY ILLUSTRATOR DON PUNCHATZ FOR AN UNPUBLISHED TIME MAGAZINE COVER.

LIFE ON TATOOINE: LUKE IS PICTURED "WASTING TIME WITH HIS FRIENDS" BIGGS AND CAMIE, RACING ACROSS THE PLAINS OF THE DESERT PLANET.

"Actually, the first Star Wars image I ever saw was Threepio walking past the monster skeleton in the desert, and that desert made a real impression on me," recalls illustrator MICHAEL ALLRED, who arrived at his local movie theater about 20 minutes into Star Wars. Color by DANNY HELLMAN.

Is it Anakin Skywalker on the funeral pyre...or Darth Vader? "Both" Luke Skywalker is probably thinking as he contemplates the passing of his father.

"I always wondered what Luke was thinking in this scene," reflects illustrator MATT HALEY. "He's respecting his nemesis and saying good-bye to his father. That's what makes Luke a hero, not all the space battles." Inks by SHEPHERD HENDRIX; color by JOHN CEBOLLERO.

Darth Vader's infamous psychic stranglehold, a running motif in the STAR WARS saga.

Illustrator WALTER MCDANIEL found himself "caught in the grip" of Lord Vader's powerful influence. Inks by RICH BUCKLER JR.; color by JOHN CEBOLLERO.

AN UNATTRIBUTED CONCEPT PAINTING FOR *THE EMPIRE STRIKES BACK* PRESENTS A SOMEWHAT STYLIZED, IMPOSING CLOSE-UP OF DARTH VADER.

THIS GOUACHE PAINTING BY BRITISH ILLUSTRATOR JOHN B. HIGGINS APPEARED ON THE COVER OF ONE OF MARVEL'S *THE EMPIRE STRIKES BACK* MONTHLIES IN THE U.K.

THE FATHER/SON CONFLICT OF *STAR WARS*, NEVER MORE IMAGINATIVELY ILLUSTRATED. LUKE IS INDEED THE INHERITOR OF HIS FATHER'S AWESOME POWERS AND POTENTIAL. BUT WILL SKYWALKER'S SON ONE DAY SUCCUMB TO THE DARK SIDE OF THE FORCE?

"I've always written stories about father and son relationships, and thought that having Luke Skywalker in a scene with Darth Vader would be very moving and appropriate, the late JACK KIRBY said of his illustration. Artist/writer Kirby changed the look of comic books with his cinematically powerful graphics and non-stop ability to create new characters, concepts and genres. Inks by MICHAEL THIBODEAUX; color by JANET JACKSON.

MIRAN KIM © 93

And in this moment, a boy becomes a man: after discovering the charred remains of his aunt and uncle, Luke resolves to learn the ways of the Force and become a Jedi like his father. It is a scene of unsparing shock; the turning point in young Skywalker's destiny.

"The scene where Luke finds his family brutally murdered by the stormtroopers still haunts me,"

reveals illustrator MIRAN KIM. "The aftermath of man's continuing inhumanity to man, is the energy of anger, powerlessness, and the lust for revenge. If we truly want to succeed and fight to see who can shine brightest, we must castrate ourselves in voice; be emotional self-censors to win the struggle for belonging."

A thrilling scene from *Return of the Jedi* featured on a lunch box from the Thermos Company. It was rendered by East Coast advertising artist GENE LEMERY.

UKE SKYWALKER IN THE PRIMORDIAL SWAMPSCAPE OF DAGOBAH, AS PRESENTED IN *THE EMPIRE STRIKES BACK*.

"I've spent a lot of time in the South...in Florida exploring swamps, catching snakes...even catching alligators with a rope!" recalls illustrator *ARTHUR SUYDAM*, whose art frequently reflects a fascination for things reptilian.

A*LLIES IN EVIL:* GRAND MOFF TARKIN AND DARTH VADER CALLING THE SHOTS FROM THEIR FULLY-OPERATIONAL BATTLE STATION. TARKIN'S LINES OF DIALOGUE ARE AMONG THE MOST QUOTABLE IN THE SAGA.

"The late Peter Cushing was fabulous as Tarkin and was a great subject to draw," offers illustrator *KELLEY JONES*. Color by *LES DORSCHEID*.

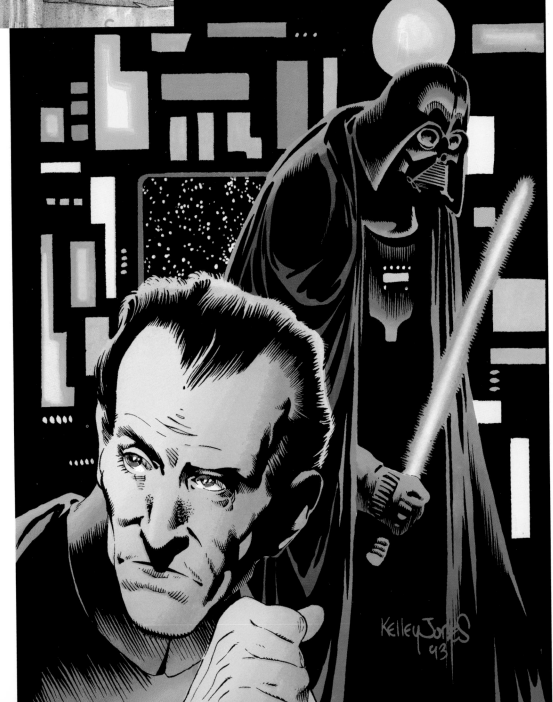

THE FACE BEHIND THE MASK: ANAKIN SKYWALKER AND HIS DARK SIDE PERSONA ON DISPLAY.

"I was most struck by the transformations of Darth Vader throughout the Star Wars saga," observes illustrator SYLVAIN. "Anakin Skywalker embodies the triumph of man over machine - a great modern myth."

"THE FORCE IS WITH YOU, YOUNG SKYWALKER, BUT YOU ARE NOT A JEDI YET": LUKE'S FIRST CONFRONTATION WITH DARTH VADER IN THE CLOUD CITY OF BESPIN.

"Upon receiving this assignment, I went out and bought a Darth Vader model kit," admits illustrator JIMMY PALMIOTTI. "I figured this was a good way to study Vader's outfit and an even better excuse to have a model of my favorite Star Wars villain." Color by RICHARD ORY.

ARTH VADER BECKONS TO HIS INJURED OFFSPRING. "TOGETHER WE CAN END THIS SENSELESS CONFLICT AND BRING ORDER TO THE GALAXY!" HE EXHORTS.

"This is the moment where Luke turns completely from the dark side," comments illustrator BRANDON PETERSON. "It is the ultimate moment in the series, as far as I'm concerned." Color by MIKE MCPHILLIPS.

Luke confronts his greatest of all enemies in one of Master Yoda's tests on Dagobah. Luke seeing his own face within Vader's helmet suggest disturbing discoveries to come.

"I dunno, but if the Jedi Master who trained Obi-Wan Kenobi told me, 'Your weapons, you will not need them', I'd like to think I'd leave 'em behind," observes illustrator RAY LAGO. "It makes ya wonder what Luke would have found in the cave if he'd entered unarmed."

VADER ADDRESSES THE HOLOGRAPHIC IMAGE OF EMPEROR PALPATINE IN THIS CLASSIC MOMENT FROM *THE EMPIRE STRIKES BACK*. BRITISH ACTOR CLIVE REVILL PROVIDED THE EMPEROR'S VOICE.

"*Star Wars has incredible-looking villains, heroes, a love story, adventure, humor, special effects... no wonder we all went nuts when we first saw it!*" observes illustrator NELSON. Color by RICHARD ORY.

THE EMPEROR RENAMING ANAKIN SKYWALKER AS LORD DART

A PORTRAIT OF THE EVIL EMPEROR PALPATINE AS HE APPEARS IN *RETURN OF THE JEDI*. ACTOR IAN MCDIARMID PLAYED THE ROLE WITH CACKLING AUTHORITY.

"Although I have not actually seen the Star Wars movies, I do love them," admits ever-offbeat illustrator DREW FRIEDMAN. "Illustrating the Emperor is the high point of my career. Thank you all." Color by JOHN CEBOLLERO.

A NAKIN SKYWALKER IS ABOUT TO BECOME LORD DARTH VADER IN THIS APPROPRIATE-LY DARK CEREMONY PRESIDED OVER BY EMPEROR PALPATINE FLANKED BY HIS IMPERIAL GUARDS.

"I thought of this piece as a kind of flip side to the sacred cere-mony of knighthood," explains illustrator THOM ANG. "I made it a dark, solemn affair—a tragic transformation."

Enough is enough! After witnessing Palpatine's devastating psychic assault on Luke, Darth Vader turns on the evil Emperor and hurls him to his doom.

"It's a very dramatic moment in Return of the Jedi," observes illustrator HOANG NGUYEN. "Vader forsakes the dark side, even though it costs him his life." Color by RICHARD ORY.

An illustration of the redeemed Anakin Skywalker from the Libby Perszyk Kathman Studio. It was used to promote an action figure of Anakin issued by Kenner. From the collection of Thomas H. Neiheisel.

This exceptional painting by Bill Sienkiewicz appeared on the cover of Marvel's *Return of the Jedi* comics adaptation back in 1983. Sienkiewicz rendered an equally breathtaking 'New Visions' card for the first series of *Star Wars Galaxy*.

CHAPTER FOUR

ALL CREATURES GREAT & ALIEN

Memorable movie creatures were in short supply back in the mid-70's. We had endured an uneven run of *Planet of the Apes* sequels, *The Exorcist* (with its pioneering make-up effects) had come and gone, and something new and unsavory—the "slasher" school of horror film—was just beginning its long, unlamented run.

But an outrageous, unearthly, head-to-claw, honest-to-gosh alien creature—that kind of character hadn't

been seen since the heyday of the 1950's sci-fi chiller. Lucas reached even further back for inspiration, way back to classic mythology, then a little further ahead to the flamboyant pulp magazine covers of the '30s and '40s. In the end, *Star Wars* was a homage to all great sci-fi creatures of the past—a celebration of extraterrestrial strangeness—with the various monstrosities supporting the film's plot, not stealing the spotlight.

Except, of course, for one particular sequence set in a Mos Eisley watering hole.

"George Lucas and I talked at length about the cantina sequence and the different alien concepts. We both had a lot of fun being so enthusiastic about the film," recalls award-winning make-up artist Rick Baker, who contributed several odd-looking life forms to the scene. "I did four!" notes fellow monster-manufacturer Laine Liska with unabashed pride. "When you go into the barroom, I did the first character you see. It was sort of a T-headed guy with glowing eyes. There was a Cyclops-like thing; another one resembled a goat; still another was a big, white furry guy with four eyes. I got to play 'him' in the movie.

Actually, all of us who worked on them managed to get into the act. I even got a laugh—I'm the guy who scratches his head!"

Adds Doug Beswick: "We did thirteen different aliens and I did seven of one particular head for that band. Rick Baker donated several of his masks that he already had made. Whatever was available we used to fill up the barroom and the old masks really helped." Monsters from the Baker stu-

OPPOSITE PAGE, CLOCKWISE: A NEVER-DEVELOPED "WRETCHED SOUL" CONCEIVED BY JOE JOHNSTON; JEDI MASTER YODA, AS PRESENTED IN THE EMPIRE STRIKES BACK; A TUSKEN RAIDER (OR SAND PERSON) POSES MENACINGLY FOR THIS STAR WARS PUBLICITY SHOT. THIS PAGE, BELOW: THE ALWAYS-REMARKABLE "HAMMERHEAD" FROM STAR WARS' CANTINA SEQUENCE. HE WAS QUITE A STARTLING SIGHT BACK IN '77.

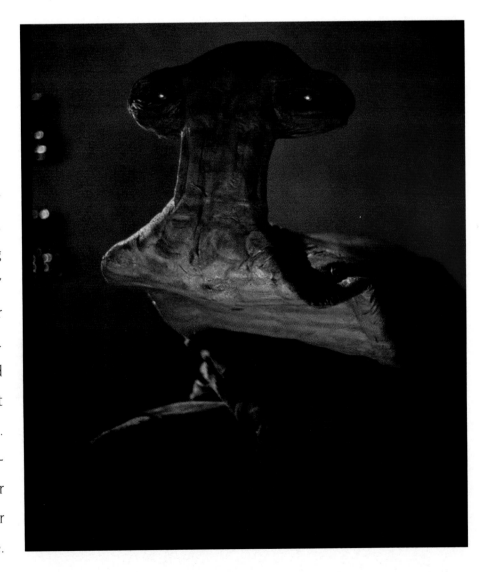

dio were added to creatures originally conceived in England, such as Stuart Freeborn's popular Greedo.

The cantina sequence proved to be one of the most popular set pieces from Star Wars. Two movies later, Lucas would rework the concept and expand it into the ultimate, over-the-top creature feast. "I was never completely satisfied with the cantina scene," he admits. "By the time we got to Jedi, we had the time and the resources to do it pretty much the way I originally envisioned it." This resulted in Jabba the Hutt's throne room follies, a collection of the wildest

TOP RIGHT: A MULTI-ORBED CANTINA DENIZEN—HE'S THE ONE WHO SCRATCHES HIS HEAD—FROM THE ORIGINAL STAR WARS. BELOW: A NIGHTMARISH EMPEROR PALPATINE, DEVELOPED BY NILO RODIS-JAMERO AND AGGIE GUERARD RODGERS.

extraterrestrial low-lifers ever assembled on the motion picture screen. Jabba himself was a massive, Sydney Greenstreet-type slug of a gangster with a insatiable appetite and a deep, hearty laugh. His Royal Immenseness, another Stuart Freeborn creation, was composed of two tons of clay and 600 pounds of latex.

Not all of the aliens created for the saga were supporting characters. In addition to Chewie and, to a lesser extent, Admiral Ackbar, Yoda (performed by Frank Oz) was an astonishing achievement in his day. Introduced in *The Empire Strikes Back*, the diminutive Jedi master was given "Albert

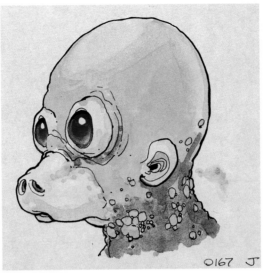

A PAIR OF BIZARRE, NEVER-EMPLOYED CREATURE DESIGNS BY NILO RODIS-JAMERO (LEFT) AND JOE JOHNSTON (RIGHT). BELOW: JABBA THE HUTT HOLDING COURT, AS PRESENTED IN RETURN OF THE JEDI. AN EARLIER, LESS AMBITIOUS VERSION OF JABBA WAS ORIGINALLY SLATED TO APPEAR IN THE FIRST STAR WARS MOVIE.

Einstein eyes" by his creator, Stuart Freeborn, and pushed state-of-the-art puppetry to a new high.

We can only wonder what the producer and his creative cohorts have up their sleeves for future *Star Wars* films. Certainly that galaxy far, far away is inhabited by myriad alien races; we've only seen a handful. With computer-generated imagery and other newly-developed, high-tech special effects and make-up, the possibilities are as limitless as the imaginations of the artists, designers and technicians involved. The most amazing gargoyles may be yet to come!

AN ENRAGED GAMORREAN GUARD THUNDERS TOWARD US, SKULLS RATTLING IN HIS WAKE. GEORGE LUCAS REFERRED TO THESE CREATURES AS "THE PIGS", OR "PIG-GUARDS".

"I was under the impression that I was being paid by the pound, so I simply choose the most obese character I could find!" laughs illustrator RICH HEDDEN (say Rich, didn't you notice Jabba?). Inks and color by MIKE McPHILLIPS.

ANOTHER GAMORREAN GUARD, THIS ONE APPARENTLY DESIGNATED THE RANCOR'S KEEPER, FEEDS THE FEARSOME CREATURE IN THE PIT BELOW JABBA THE HUTT'S THRONE ROOM.

"The rancor is an excellent-looking monster," opines illustrator FRANK BRUNNER. "As a matter of fact, he's probably my favorite creature in the Star Wars universe. I even bought the model kit!"

PORTRAIT OF AN UGNAUGHT: ONE OF THOSE GROSS LITTLE BEASTIES GLIMPSED TOSSING THREEPIO'S HEAD ABOUT IN *THE EMPIRE STRIKES BACK.*

"For my Galaxy trading card, I chose to stay away from the familiar Star Wars characters," explains illustrator MARSHALL ARISMAN. "I settled on an Ugnaught, one of those little pig-like creature glimpsed briefly in Empire."

SEAN - I'M WORKING UP A "SALACIOUS CARD - 27451 ZECK

JABBA THE HUTT'S COURT WAS FILLED WITH SOME OF THE WILDEST AND MOST OUTRAGEOUS CREATURES IN THE GALAXY - THE ULTIMATE MONSTER MASH. ESPECIALLY MEMORABLE WAS EVER-CACKLING SALACIOUS CRUMB, SEEN HERE ESCAPING R2-D2'S ELECTRICAL DISCHARGE IN THE PRISON BARGE SEQUENCE OF *RETURN OF THE JEDI.*

"I like muppet-like characters, especially ones with maniacal little laughs," offers illustrator MIKE ZECK. "And it's only in the barge scene that we get to see his body." Color by RICHARD ORY.

VARIOUS MEMBERS OF JABBA THE HUTT'S INFAMOUS COURT OF OTHER-WORLDLY CREATURES. LUCAS HOPED TO TOP HIS OWN CANTINA SCENE FROM *STAR WARS* WITH THIS POPULAR *JEDI* SET-PIECE.

"I originally wanted to draw Peter Cushing, but he was taken,"

explains illustrator BOB FINGER-MAN. "So I figured I'd go the polar opposite end of the spectrum and draw something short, squat and silly, instead of tall, gaunt and daunting."

AN OBESE FEMALE WHO OBVIOUSLY ADORES PARTYING, YARNA WAS SEEN ONLY BRIEFLY IN *JEDI*'S JABBA THE HUTT SEQUENCE.

"I tried a couple of different characters from this scene, and Yarna worked right away," explains illustrator JANINE JOHNSTON. "She just seemed so happy, dancing around...guess I've always enjoyed fat, happy people."

A GROTESQUE, UNNAMED BOUNTY HUNTER TAKES TIME OUT FROM HIS DANGEROUS WORK TO POSE WITH VARIOUS WEAPONS—ONE OF WHICH HAS RECENTLY BEEN USED.

"There is so much conflict in the Star Wars universe," offers illustrator TIM BRADSTREET, that it isn't surprising that bounty hunters abound. They come in all shapes and sizes...and are always sinister-looking.

AN UNGUARDED MOMENT FROM *RETURN OF THE JEDI*: THE AFTERMATH OF THE PRISON BARGE BATTLE ON TATOOINE.

"I wanted to convey the bitterness after the storm," relates illustrator JOHN PAUL LONA. "There are two Weequay in (Jedi)—identical, except they're dressed differently—and during the battle they get thrown off the skiff, or one is throttled by Luke's lightsaber. The other one survives, and will possibly seek revenge in the future..." Color by REBECCA GUAY.

Those ferocious nomads of Tatooine, the Tusken Raiders (also known as "Sand People").

"I've always wondered about the culture and background of the Tusken Raiders," comments illustrator TIM TRUMAN. "Are they indigenous to Tatooine? Maybe we'll find out in the next trilogy..."

A number of rancors on Tatooine are herded by spaceships in this imaginary scene.

"There is a certain sadness to the rancor, even when he's attacking Luke," observes illustrator RON BROWN. "Some believe him to be a mutant, the only one of his kind. I chose a different origin. Here we see poachers flying in, to abduct one of the young rancors for a black market sale to Jabba the Hutt."

THREEPIO IN BONDAGE: CAPTURED BY JAWAS, HE IS LED ACROSS THE STEAMING PLAINS OF TATOOINE TO THEIR SAND-CRAWLER.

"No doubt he's complaining as usual!" laughs illustrator DAVE GIBBONS. "It's great to get a chance to do something connected to Star Wars. I've loved it since I went to a press preview, way back in 1977, and sat open-mouth throughout." Color by JOHN CEBOLLERO.

ANOTHER, ESPECIALLY TERRIFYING VIEW OF JABBA'S PET MONSTER, THE RANCOR. VARIOUS SPECIAL EFFECTS TECHNIQUES WERE ATTEMPTED TO BRING HIM TO SCREEN LIFE—INCLUDING A FULL-SIZED COSTUME. ULTIMATELY, ADVANCED PUPPETRY DID THE TRICK.

"Star Wars is a great movie with great special effects and great spaceships and cool aliens," concludes illustrator JAE LEE. "I think it'll be a hit." Color by RICHARD : ORY

IN THE *MILLENNIUM FALCON*, CHEWBACCA AND THREEPIO KEEP THIER MINDS ON THE HOLOBOARD GAME...AND THE GROTESQUE LITTLE CREATURES THAT BRING THEIR MOVES TO LIFE.

"This scene was funny, but there was an undercurrent of brutality to it," observes illustrator *RICK GEARY*, who reminds us that it's not wise to upset a Wookiee. *"I also debated about whether I should make the characters more transparent. I finally decided not to."*

GETTING WRAPPED UP IN HIS WORK: THE MUSCIAL MR. McCOOL FINDS HIMSELF ENVELOPED BY BEAUTIFUL OOLA, JABBA THE HUTT'S DANCING SLAVE GIRL (AND EVENTUALLY ONE OF THE RANCOR'S SNACKS).

"Take five Droopy!" says illustrator *LINDA MEDLEY.*

ONE OF THE MOST CHARMING ELEMENTS OF THE *STAR WARS* SAGA IS THE CONCEPT OF THROWAWAY MOMENTS; LITTLE THINGS HAPPENING IN THE CORNER OF THE FRAME OR MAYBE JUST OUT OF CAMERA RANGE THAT RESONATE GREATLY. ONE SUCH MOMENT, FROM *RETURN OF THE JEDI*, IS VISUALIZED HERE.

"I like the serious mythological themes in Star Wars, but I also love the humor," comments illus-

trator DAVID O. MILLER.

"Especially the Worrt (the frog-like road creature from Jedi). "He sees, he eats, he belches."

ONE OF THE MOST RESPECTED FANTASY ILLUSTRATORS OF ALL TIME, MICHAEL WHELAN, JOINED FORCES WITH ONE OF THE MOST RESPECTED FANTASY FILMMAKERS OF ALL TIME, GEORGE LUCAS. THIS COMBINATION OF IMAGINATIVE TALENT LED TO THE CREATION OF A CLASSIC WHELAN PAINTING: THE JEDI MASTER YODA IN A CONTEMPLATIVE MOOD. WHELAN RENDERED A NUMBER OF PENCIL PRELIMS—QUITE BREATHTAKING IN THEIR OWN RIGHT—BEFORE BEGINNING THE ACTUAL ILLUSTRATION. IT WAS ULTIMATELY USED AS THE COVER OF A DIARY, "MY JEDI JOURNAL." (FROM THE COLLECTION OF WILLIAM PLUMB)

On the ice planet of Hoth, Luke Skywalker uses the Force to escape from captivity and eventually clashes with his abductor, the monstrous snow creature know as the Wampa.

"Imagine if each and every scene in the Star Wars saga had been filmed from 100 different angles," suggests illustrator MARK PACELLA, who adds, "I have always wanted my very own lightsaber." Inks by ART THIBERT; color by JOHN CEBOLLERO.

Portrait of a wampa: the abominable snow creature of Hoth in all his terrifying glory.

"There are really two wampas," explains illustrator RICARDO DELGADO. "One of them has horns coming out of his forehead, the other one (glimpsed in close-up at the beginning of the film) doesn't. The one with the horns is a lot cooler, so I grabbed that one [for my illustration]."

LUKE'S LEVITATED POV, IN THE MIDST OF HIS JEDI TRAINING ON DAGOBAH (AS PRESENTED IN THE EMPIRE STRIKES BACK). NOTE THAT SEVERAL OBJECTS—INCLUDING R2-D2—ARE HOVERING ABOVE YODA.

"Beyond the inspiration of the Star Wars movie trilogy, The Art of Star Wars books really sent me into orbit," remembers illustrator DAVID LOWERY. "(These creations) continue to stand as the high watermark of what artistic vision can bring to the movies."

JEDI MASTER YODA, THE CURIOUS LITTLE GNOME WHO FIRST TAUGHT OBI-WAN KENOBI THE WAYS OF THE FORCE, THEN LATER DID THE SAME FOR LUKE SKYWALKER.

"I like the way Yoda carried himself," comments illustrator WHILCE PORTACIO. "He didn't get into the hype and the glory of his achievements. Sure, he could do wonderful things with his powers, but he only did things that mattered. He was a real hero."

THIS STARTLING PORTRAIT OF A TUSKEN RAIDER WAS RENDERED BY BASIL GOGOS, AN ACCOMPLISHED ILLUSTRATOR PERHAPS BEST KNOW FOR HIS SEMINAL FAMOUS MONSTERS OF FILMLAND MAGAZINE COVERS. GOGOS USES DRAMATIC LIGHTING AND PROVOCATIVE COLOR SCHEMES THAT COMMAND THE VIEWER'S ATTENTION. THIS PAINTING WAS PRINTED ON THE COVER OF A 1978 ISSUE OF FAMOUS MONSTERS. FROM THE COLLECTION OF WILLIAM PLUMB.

YODA WAS AN ODDLY LOGICAL CHOICE TO APPEAR ON A LUCASFILM CHRISTMAS CARD. RALPH McQUARRIE PRODUCED A FEW VARIATIONS: ONE HAD THE LITTLE JEDI MASTER IN A SLEIGH FILLED WITH HOLIDAY GIFTS. "I REALLY WASN'T A SCIENCE FICTION BUFF AT ALL," ADMITS McQUARRIE. "THAT'S THE ODD THING ABOUT MY INVOLVEMENT IN STAR WARS, BECAUSE THE MOVIE WAS REALLY THIS GREAT, MOVING SCIENCE FICTION ILLUSTRATION."

INDUSTRIAL LIGHT & MAGIC ILLUSTRATOR NILO RODIS-JAMERO PRODUCED HUNDREDS OF ALIEN AND CREATURE DESIGNS FOR *RETURN OF THE JEDI*, INCLUDING THE LARGE-SNOUTED ENTITIES VISUALIZED HERE.

BEFORE JOINING ILM, RODIS-JAMERO DESIGNED HEAVY INDUSTRIAL VEHICLES, INCLUDING MILITARY TANKS, WHICH WAS EXCELLENT BASIC TRAINING FOR HIS *STAR WARS* WORK.

JOE JOHNSTON, THE ART DIRECTOR OF VISUAL EFFECTS FOR *RETURN OF THE JEDI*, PRODUCED THIS WHIMSICAL ILLUSTRATION OF AN EWOK.

IN THIS DETAILED SKETCH BY CONCEPT ARTIST/DESIGNER JOE JOHNSTON, AN EWOK SCOUTING PARTY MAKES USE OF SOME STRANGE BEASTS OF BURDEN. ALTHOUGH THE LITTLE EWOKS WERE A PRIMITIVE RACE, THEIR LACK OF TECHNOLOGY WAS COMPENSATED FOR BY THEIR SHREWDNESS AND TACTICAL SKILLS.

AN EARLY DESIGN OF THE WAMPA FROM *THE EMPIRE STRIKES BACK*, RENDERED BY JOE JOHNSTON. THE CREATURE BECAME A LOT SHAGGIER AND WHITER, BUT NO LESS FEROCIOUS. JOHNSTON PRODUCED COUNTLESS STORYBOARDS AND SKETCHES FOR ILM, WHICH HE JOINED TWO WEEKS OUT OF COLLEGE.

CHAPTER FIVE

TWO OF A KIND: HAN & CHEWIE

Every hero needs a sidekick. It's an endearing tradition dating back to the earliest days of adventure fiction. Ever since spacebuckler Han Solo rescued the Wookiee Chewbacca from Imperial enslavement, these two have been inseparable. Which is curious, since Wookiees on the whole appear to be creatures who prefer sticking to their own species.

"I wanted a relationship with (Chewbacca) that would imply trust and equality," states Han Solo himself, actor Harrison Ford. It started out as a boy-and-his-dog kind of idea, but the concept evolved. As did the Wookiees themselves.

"Originally, they were much more primitive," explains George Lucas, who initially envisioned an army of the furry giants overwhelming Imperial forces during the saga's climax. "But once we established Chewie as a fairly sophisticated character, we couldn't do that anymore. So, we invented the Ewoks."

It was artist/designer Ralph McQuarrie who first played around with Chewbacca's simian appearance. "George was talking about a 'lemur look', some kind of large furry creature with lemur eyes. So I did some really

big apelike characters, huge and muscular, sort of super-hero types...but with this lemur face, with all kinds of bandoleers of ammunition and so forth strapped around his body." Ultimately, it was resident make-up wizard Stuart Freeborn who fine-tuned Chewbacca into the relatively handsome Wookiee we know today.

But finding a voice for Chewie—indeed, developing a Wookiee language of sorts—proved to be an equally complicated task. Unlike other *Star Wars* creatures, Chewbacca had to act and appear in various scenes with

HAN SOLO (HARRISON FORD) AND CHEWBACCA (PETER MAYHEW)—SPACE PIRATES-TURNED-REBEL HEROES. TOP: A CAPTURED HAN IS ABOUT TO BARBECUED BY EWOKS IN RETURN OF THE JEDI. LEFT: CHEWBACCA DONS A BREATH MASK WHILE CHECKING OUT A SUPPOSED ASTEROID CAVE IN THE EMPIRE STRIKES BACK.

the other actors. He certainly couldn't speak English, or any other recognizably "human" language on record.

"(George Lucas) had a recording of bears grunting and making vocalizations," recalls sound effects supervisor Ben Burtt, who spent an entire year recording preliminary sounds for Star Wars. "(During that time) I collected lots of bear sounds, as well as walruses, and lions, and badgers, and sick animals, and all sorts of things. Out of all those recordings you could extract little bits of sound: little grunts and moans and ughs and arggs, even purring sounds, and they all had certain emotional feelings associated with them. So I tried cutting these together to try to get a sense of speech out of Chewie."

Eventually cast as towering Chewbacca was 7' 2" Peter Mayhew, previously the monstrous Minoton in Ray Harryhausen's *Sinbad and the Eye of the Tiger*. Although conditions in the one-piece, yak and mohaired costume were difficult, "I soon got used to the heat," Mayhew remembers.

And what about Chewie's other half, that handsome-if-scruffy-looking, devil-may-care space adventurer Han Solo?

"(Harrison Ford) started out in *American Graffiti*," recalls George Lucas, "and then I used him as a foil to do tests on *Star Wars*. He was brought in to play against the other actors, I had all these Lukes coming in... And when you watched the screen tests of Harrison playing (Solo) and the other actors playing the role, there was no question he was the best."

The rest, as they say, is celluloid history. Han and Chewie (or is it Harrison and Peter?) have undeniable screen chemistry and a rapport that is somewhat indefinable. The bottom line is Solo may be a big brother to Luke and the apple of Princess Leia's eye, but his best pal is—and will always remain—a certain Wookiee named Chewbacca.

THE CHARACTER OF CHEWBACCA WAS INSPIRED BY GEORGE LUCAS' PET, A LARGE FURRY MALAMUTE DOG NAMED INDIANA. HAN SOLO WAS SQUARELY IN THE PULP-INSPIRED TRADITION OF DEVIL-MAY-CARE SPACE HEROES.

HAN SOLO FACES SOME NAMELESS HOR-
ROR ON AN UNDISCLOSED, IF PICTURESQUE,
PLANET.

"*Since* Star Wars *is part of the
'space fantasy' adventure genre,*"
observes illustrator DAN BARRY, "*I
decided, as a kind of 'in' joke, to
put Han Solo in a Flash Gordon-
like situation and setting.*" Color
by MIKE McPHILLIPS.

THAT DYNAMIC DUO OF THE STARWAYS, HAN AND CHEWIE, ARE ONCE AGAIN EMBROILED IN IMPERIAL ENTANGLEMENTS. CHEWBACCA IS PICTURED WITH HIS CROSS-BOW, NEVER ACTUALLY USED IN THE FILMS.

"Chewbacca was once rescued from Imperial slavery by Han Solo," explains illustrator C. SCOTT MORSE. "Here, Chewie is seen repaying his Wookiee life-debt by saving his companion from certain doom."

TORTURED BY THE EMPIRE: A CAPTURED HAN SOLO IS STRAPPED INTO AN EXOTIC CHAIR AND GIVEN 'THE TREATMENT' BY LORD VADER'S STORMTROOPERS.

"I thought Han's torture scene would be cool (to render) 'cause I could draw teeth and spittle!!" offers illustrator GREG CAPULLO with a Jabba-like glint in his eye. Color by JOHN CEBOLLERO.

A WHIMSICAL VIEW OF CHEWBACCA IN HIS "SHOP" (NOTE THE "HIS" AND "HERS" BATHROOM KEYS ON THE FAR RIGHT).

"I heard Chewbacca is a great mechanic," muses illustrator AMANDA CONNER. "Maybe on his home planet he has a shop or a service station. Incidentally, my parents used to know Harrison Ford when he was a carpenter. He and my dad pulled, like 6,000,000 nails from an old floor at our house. We still have his old miter box." Color by MIKE McPHILLIPS.

CONCEPT ARTIST JOE JOHNSTON RENDERED THESE WOOKIEE-THEMED ILLUSTRATIONS FOR THE STAR WARS HOLIDAY SPECIAL (CBS), BROADCAST ON THANKSGIVING BACK IN 1978. ALTHOUGH THE SPECIAL ITSELF WAS CONSIDERED DISAPPOINTING, A NELVANA-PRODUCED ANIMATED SHORT INTRODUCING BOBA FETT (SEE PAGE 117) WAS FEATURED, AS WAS AN EXTENDED VISIT WITH CHEWBACCA'S FAMILY. IN ONE IDEA FOR THE SHOW, CHEWIE AND SON LUMPY EXPERIENCE A VIRTUAL REALITY RIDE.

ENVIRONMENTAL TRANSPORTER ②

ENVIRONMENTAL TRANSPORTER ④

HAN SOLO AND CHEWBACCA HAVE AN AUDIENCE WITH THE GALAXY'S MOST NOTORIOUS GANGSTER, JABBA THE HUTT. "WITH SO MANY INTERESTING-LOOKING CRITTERS IN THE WHOLE JABBA SEQUENCE, THE PROBLEM FOR AN ARTIST IS NOT SO MUCH WHAT TO PUT IN AS WHAT TO LEAVE OUT," EXPLAINS ILLUSTRATOR RALPH REESE. "HERE WE SEE SMUGGLER SOLO SMOOTH-TALKING HIS WAY INTO A BIG LOAN FROM THE INTERSTELLAR LOAN SHARK/GANGSTER, WHICH HE SOMEHOW NEVER GETS AROUND TO REPAYING."

SOMETIMES AN ILLUSTRATION REVEALS A GOOD DEAL MORE ABOUT THE CHARACTERS IT'S DEPICTING BY NOT ACTUALLY SHOWING THE CHARACTERS' FACES.

"I chose to depict a key moment in the relationship between Han and Chewie," explains illustrator JASON PEARSON. "Han rescues the Wookiee from enslavement and then burns his Imperial 'draft card.' It's a scene that isn't shown in any of the movies, of course, but it is part of the back story of Star Wars." Color by MIKE McPHILLIPS.

AS LEIA AND THREEPIO LOOK ON ANXIOUSLY, HAN SOLO AND CHEWBACCA PUSH THE *MILLENNIUM FALCON* TO ITS LIMITS. EAST COAST ADVERTISING ILLUSTRATOR GENE LEMERY STRIKES AGAIN WITH ANOTHER DAZZLING PAINTING THAT APPEARED ON A LUNCH BOX FOR THE THERMOS COMPANY. THERE WERE A DOZEN DIFFERENT *RETURN OF THE JEDI* METAL AND PLASTIC LUNCH BOXES SOLD IN THE U.S. ALONE, WITH VARIATIONS OF DESIGN SOLD INTERNATIONALLY. FROM THE COLLECTION OF WILLIAM PLUMB.

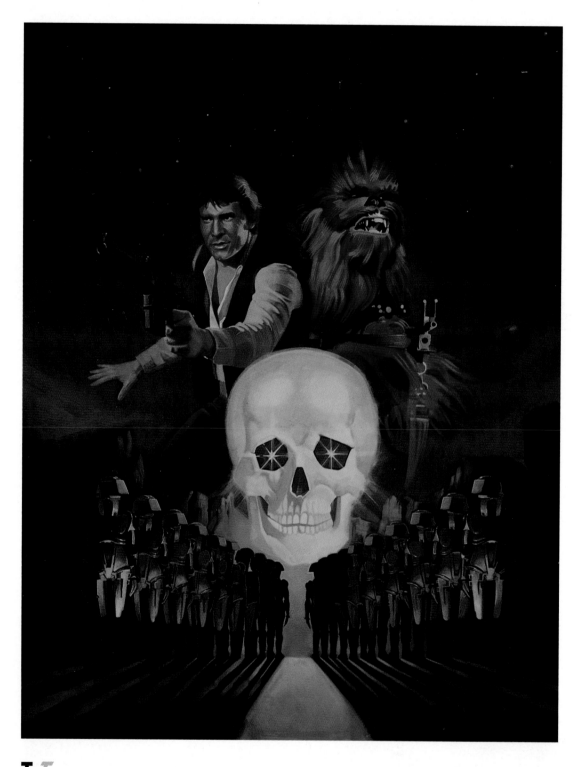

THE PRICE OF UPSETTING A WOOKIEE: HAN SOLO'S SEMI-SERIOUS WARNING COMES TO IMAGINARY LIFE WHEN CHEWBACCA LOSES HIS COOL DURING A HOLOBOARD GAME.

"To me, Star Wars *is about friendship*," observes illustrator JOE PHILLIPS. "Han Solo and Chewbacca are a classic example of two people from different backgrounds uniting for a common cause in the name of friendship."

THIS MAGNIFICENT PAINTING BY BILL SCHMIDT APPEARED AS THE COVER OF *HAN SOLO AND THE LOST LEGACY*, A *STAR WARS* PAPERBACK. TAPPING INTO HIS CREATIVE INGENUITY, SCHMIDT USED A FRENCH FOOD PROCESSOR TO MODEL THE TROOPERS. FIGURES OF HAN SOLO AND CHEWBACCA WERE BASED ON PHOTOS FROM THE ORIGINAL FILM. A DRAMATIC SKULL REPLACED THE MASK OF DARTH VADER WHEN PERMISSION WASN'T GRANTED TO USE THE DARK LORD'S IMAGE. (FROM THE COLLECTION OF WILLIAM PLUMB)

CHAPTER SIX

HEAVY METAL

The futuristic yet classical universe conceived by George Lucas is filled with machines: robots, spacecraft, exotic vehicles and weaponry, even soldiers in metallic costumes that make them look like machines.

"The idea of a 'used' future was George's," recalls Mechanical Effects Supervisor John Stears. "He was very strong on that point. We sat through a

lot of movies to get that basic feeling. We saw westerns, classics and would you believe, *Fellini Satyricon*?"

In previous science fiction epics, all the hardware looked shiny and new —which it was, since fortunes were spent creating these props and the producers couldn't wait to "show them off." But Lucas knew he was creating something unique in *Star Wars*. For the fantasy to work, it would have to be credible on its own terms. Given the battering the various vehicles and droids were subjected to, it was only

logical for their metallic surfaces to appear tarnished, discolored or dented.

"My sketches (of C-3PO) originally were of this very smooth and elegant figure, which I kind of liked," reflects concept designer Ralph McQuarrie. "But I was wrong, because he wouldn't have had the personality that he needed to have. There's something about those big round eyes (developed and refined by John Barry) that gives him a sort of astonished, comical look..."

As for R2-D2, McQuarrie designed a "cylinder with a dome on top," partially to differentiate the little droid from the square-shaped worker robots featured in *Silent Running*: "I put little panels on him and places for arms to come out, since I knew he had to have a lot of gadgets. He was kind of like a Swiss Army knife."

In keeping with Lucas' romantic

THE FANTASTIC VEHICLES AND ARMORED UNIFORMS OF STAR WARS PERSONIFY THE SAGA: THEY ARE FUTURISTIC, BUT 'USED', THEIR ONCE GLEAMING METAL NOW SMUDGED AND DENTED.

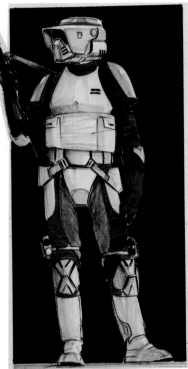

view of this galaxy, even the spaceships and war machines were "characters." Han Solo's *Millennium Falcon* (prototypes of which became the Rebel Blockade Runner!) was a true star of the Saga, and very much like its pilot: scruffy-looking, easily underestimated and unpredictable. Boba Fett's ominous craft, the *Slave* I, also reflected the character of its captain. Then there were the Imperial walkers, or AT-AT, the unforgettable metal behemoths of *The Empire Strikes Back.* "Part of the idea behind the slowness of their movements is that they could be overpowered," explains Visual Effects Supervisor Ken Ralston. "They were big, lumbering, obsolete machines."

ELEGANTLY-DESIGNED STARSHIPS AND MARCHING TANK-LIKE BEHEMOTHS (INCLUDING THE TWO-LEGGED "CHICKEN" WALKER) SUGGEST THE RANGE OF CHARACTER ATTAINABLE IN A MACHINE.

AN IMPERIAL STAR DESTROYER CLOSES IN. BELOW: BORIS VALLEJO'S GALAXY TWO BOX ART, ALSO USED AS OUR BOOK COVER, DEPICTING THREEPIO (PANICKING AS USUAL) AND ARTOO (EVER-RESOURCEFUL) TRAPPED IN A CORRIDOR ABLAZE WITH LASER FIRE.

Robots are robots and spaceships/war machines are constructed for specific tasks, but what of the human beings who have degenerated into souless, mechanized automatons? The *Star Wars* saga certainly had its fair share of those. Apart from the stormtroopers and Boba Fett, the classic, demonstrative example of this concept was Darth Vader himself. He was a man who let his humanity slip away, submerged within an elaborate life-support system, until his own son sensed the good remaining in him and helped him to reclaim his soul.

No more powerful metaphor exists for the theme George Lucas was trying to convey. No matter how mechanized or metallicized our society may become, in spite of all the miraculous advances of super-science, it is humanity—the real Force—that ultimately prevails.

THIS FANCIFUL ILLUSTRATION TELLS THE TALE OF HOW LUKE FASHIONED HIS SECOND JEDI KNIGHT WEAPON.

"The Star Wars movies explode with amazing visuals," observes illustrator *CHRIS SPROUSE.* *"My personal favorites are the lightsaber scenes. This (rendering) shows one mentioned, but not shown, in Return of the Jedi."* *Color by JOHN CEBOLLERO.*

ONE OF THE MORE UNUSUAL BOUNTY HUNTERS ASSEMBLED BY DARTH VADER IN *EMPIRE* (AND THAT'S SAYING A LOT), WAR DROID-TURNED-HIRED-KILLER IG-88 BLASTS HIS WAY INTO NEW ADVENTURE.

"When I first saw IG-88, I wondered what he was," recalls illustrator KARL ALTSTAETTER. "I was dying to see him in action. Fortunately, I got my chance!" Color by DEBBIE DAVID.

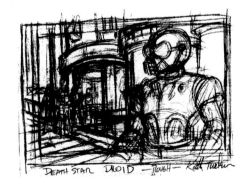

THIS INSECT-LIKE DROID CAN BE GLIMPSED IN TWO SCENES FROM THE ORIGINAL *STAR WARS*. FIRST, INSIDE THE SANDCRAWLER, THEN LATER IN THE DEATH STAR AS A "CAPTURED" CHEWIE IS ESCORTED BY "TROOPERS" HAN AND LUKE.

"I've always admired this particular droid," comments illustrator KEITH TUCKER. "He minds his own business, but you wouldn't want to mess with him." Color by JOHN CEBOLLERO.

STORMTROOPERS ARE THE NAMELESS, FACELESS—SOME SAY SOULESS—INSTRUMENTS OF MURDER IN THE SERVICE OF PALPATINE'S EVIL EMPIRE. THOUGH THERE ARE PEOPLE INSIDE THOSE WHITE-ARMORED OUTFITS, THEY LOOK AND BEHAVE MORE LIKE ROBOTS. AND YET...

"Since I was in the military, I wanted to present these guys as soldiers," explains illustrator MIKE MAYHEW. "I wanted just a taste of their humanity on display, a suggestion of real emotion as one of them begins to lose his helmet in a battle..." Color by TIER 3.

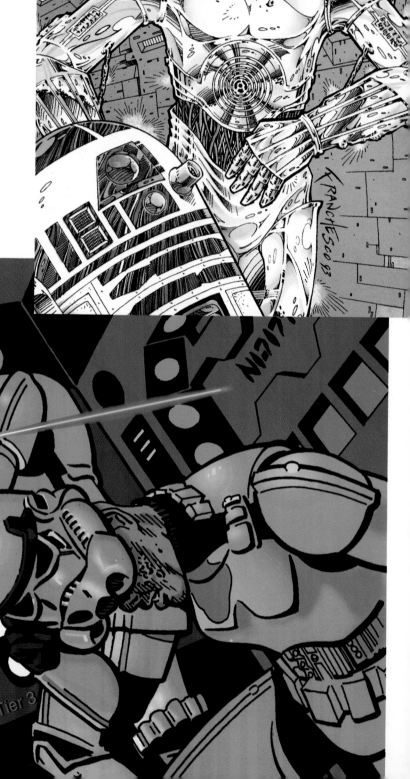

See-Threepio and Artoo-Detoo: the unlikeliest combination since Han and Chewie.

"Although R2-D2 and C-3PO were not made up of flesh and blood, they are just as real as the rest of the stellar cast," concludes illustrator FRANCHESCO. Color by JOHN CEBOLLERO.

An Imperial biker scout is attacked by four feisty Ewoks in a rendering inspired by RETURN OF THE JEDI. As all STAR WARS fans know, the diminutive Ewoks are simply inverted WOOKIEES, invented to take the place of the furry giants in the SAGA'S climax.

Although action and mayhem are continually on display in the Star Wars movies, the emphasis is on adventure, not gratuitous violence. Says illustrator JIM STARLIN: "I saw all three films and didn't climb up into a bell tower with a scoped rifle."

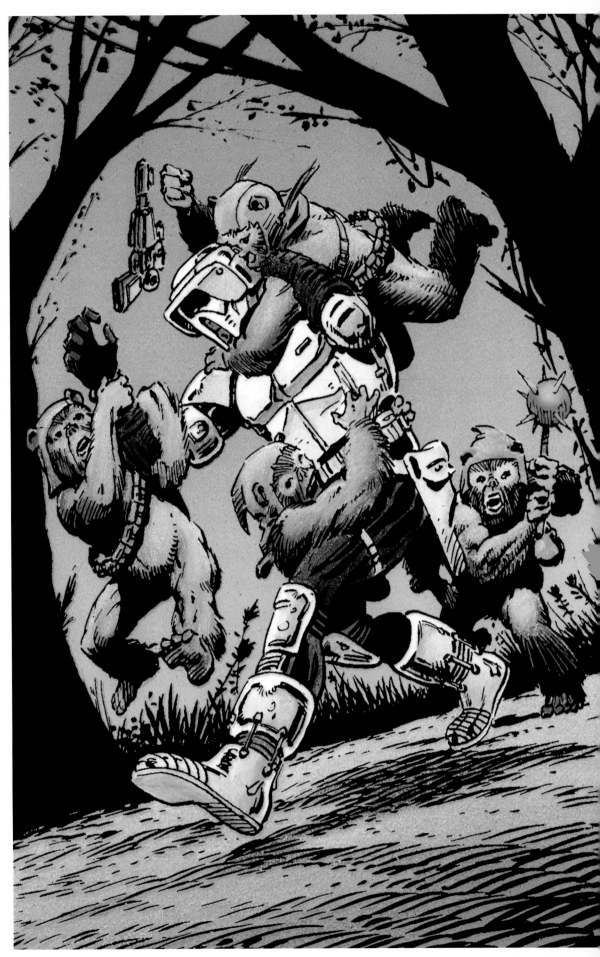

An ESPECIALLY ABSTRACT INTERPRETA-TION OF AN IMPERIAL STORMTROOPER HOLDING—YIKES!—IS THAT THREEPIO'S HEAD IN THE SOLDIER'S HAND? HE'S CER-TAINLY LOST IT BEFORE. HOPEFULLY, IT'S ANOTHER DROID WITH BIG, ROUND, PER-PETUALLY ASTONISHED EYES.

"(The stormtroopers) are super-nasty in just about any style," laughs illustrator MIKE McMAHON.

A HIGH-TECH RENDERING OF THOSE OBSOLETE-BUT-DEADLY BEHEMOTHS, THE IMPERIAL WALKERS (OR AT-AT). EMERGING FROM SNOW DRIFTS IS ONE THING; STOMPING THROUGH A POPULATED CITY IS AN ENTIRELY DIFFERENT NIGHTMARE. ORGINALLY, THE ILM TEAM TRIED BRING-ING THEM TO SCREEN LIFE THROUGH THE USE OF SOPHISTICATED PUPPETS. BUT STOP-MOTION ANIMATION PROVED THE MOST EFFECTIVE SPECIAL EFFECTS METHOD, PARTLY BECAUSE IT PRODUCED SLIGHTLY JERKY MOVEMENTS—IDEAL FOR THESE AGING, MAMMOTH SUPER-TANKS.

"The Imperial AT-ATs and Rebel Snowspeeders hold particular interest for me," explains illustra-tor NORM DWYER, who uses com-puter technology to produce his creations, *"perhaps because of their David and Goliath relation-ship."*

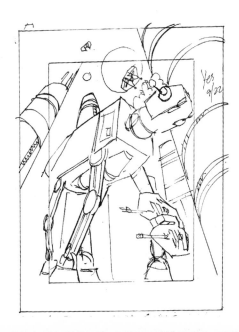

Although remembered mostly for their battle with the Ewoks in *Return of the Jedi*, at least one "Chicken" walker trundled into the Hoth sequence of *The Empire Strikes Back*. Some fans at the time mistook it for half of a blasted AT-AT, stalling about aimlessly like a chicken (walker) without a head.

"Animal-like machines fascinate me," reveals illustrator KEVIN O'NEILL. "And if they dwarf humans, I'm in (cyber) hog heaven."

DON'T MESS WITH FETT: THE INFAMOUS BOUNTY HUNTER'S EQUALLY NOTORIOUS SPACESHIP, THE *SLAVE I*, IN FULL BATTLE MODE. AFTER FETT'S DEMISE IN *JEDI*, THE VEHICLE WAS IMPOUNDED BY REBEL FORCES.

"I've always been a big Boba Fett fan," admits illustrator JOE DEVITO. *"Here, realizing he is about to be detected by an unsuspecting X-wing fighter, the ruthless bounty hunter sends it to a fiery death."*

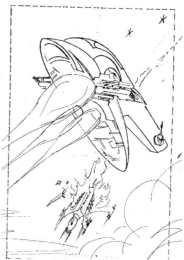

THE IMPERIAL CITY ON CORUSCANT, THE HEART OF THE EMPIRE, AS RENDERED IN 1981 BY JOE JOHNSTON. IN AN EARLY DRAFT OF *RETURN OF THE JEDI*, CORUSCANT WAS THE SITE OF A FATEFUL MEETING BETWEEN DARTH VADER AND THE EMPEROR PALPATINE. ALTHOUGH THE MAGNIFICENT CITY HAS NOT BEEN DEPICTED IN A *STAR WARS* MOVIE THUS FAR, IT MAY BE BROUGHT TO LIGHT IN A FUTURE INSTALLMENT OF THE SAGA. (FOR MORE VIEWS OF CORUSCANT, PLEASE CHECK OUT OUR RALPH MCQUARRIE CHAPTER ON PAGE 18).

WINNER OF 1993'S HUGO AWARD AS THE WORLD'S BEST SCIENCE FICTION ARTIST, DON MAITZ RENDERED THIS ENGAGING PORTRAIT OF R2-D2 FOR A *FAMOUS MONSTERS OF FILMLAND* COVER BACK IN 1977. (FROM THE COLLECTION OF WILLIAM PLUMB)

DYING OF "THIRST" ON PLANET TATOOINE: POOR THREEPIO WANDERS PAST ENORMOUS SKELETONS AS HE TREKS ACROSS THE DESERT PLAINS, ALWAYS UNDER THE WATCHFUL EYE OF ONE OF TATOOINE'S TWIN SUNS.

"I loved Star Wars *from Day One," reveals illustrator SERGIO ARAGONES. "And like any work of that magnitude, it was open for satire. I enjoyed a* MAD *look at* Star Wars *for* MAD MAGAZINE *...and I was very happy to participate in this collection."*

As a pig-guard looks on, the sadistic droid from Jabba the Hutt's torture chamber prepares something unspeakable for a new guest. "You're a fiesty one," he tells another new arrival, R2-D2.

"When I was younger and collected all those figures that Kenner Toys put out," recalls illustrator SHAWN C. MARTINBROUGH, "this particular scene stuck in my head from the Return of the Jedi collection commercial."

Admiral Ackbar, the Winston Churchill-like commander of Rebel forces in *Return of the Jedi*, commanded an equally-striking spaceship. It and others of its design resembled a lower-case "t" flying sideways. Looming in the background is the still-uncompleted Death Star, object of Rebel attack.

Although he was impressed with the ship, illustrator JEFF WATTS was even more inspired by its captain. "I've always been an admirer of Admiral Ackbar," he admits. "I'd follow him into battle anywhere!"

A PAIR OF IMPERIAL "CHICKEN" WALKERS PATROL THE FIELD.

"As a child watching (the Star Wars films), I remember being most impressed by the naturalistic movements given to the two and four-legged armored robots," says illustrator ZOHAR LAZAR. "Cunning mixing and matching of live action and stop motion animation inspired hours of imaginary play-time in my Queens, New York backyard. This memory is what fueled my interest in the famous trilogy."

DOWN AND DIRTY: ON TATOOINE, STAR-PILOT-IN-TRAINING LUKE SKYWALKER SMASHES HIS VEHICLE INTO SCRAP METAL, BUT SURVIVES TO FLY AGAIN. NOTE THE TWIN SUNS AND THE ADVENTURE'S TITLE: "STONE NEEDLE PILOTS".

"The only place that I'm aware of this scene appearing is in the Star Wars radio drama," related illustrator CULLY HAMNER. "I think it's indicative of not only Luke's youth and foolhardiness, but his strength in the Force."

CHAPTER SEVEN

A Woman's Place...

With the important exception of Princess Leia, virtually all of the characters in the original *Star Wars* were male. This is ironic since George Lucas initially expected his leading character—the one who eventually became Luke—to be a young girl.

"That was really quite a major plot change that George had to go through," Ralph McQuarrie explained in a 1977 interview. "Fox thought there

Leia Organa was certainly the highest-profile female in the Star Wars cosmos, although an occasional female Rebel could be spotted (left, from The Empire Strikes Back). Actress Carrie Fisher was 19 when she won the role of the Alderaan princess, a character who occasionally assumes exotic disguises (opposite page, lower left) in the course of her missions.

should be some romantic interest. I think this is why George made Luke a girl. Then Han Solo would be the robust hero and we could have a little tension between the two characters." McQuarrie even rendered the female "Luke" in a few concept drawings (featured in GALAXY ONE), along with what appears to be a bearded, lightsaber-brandishing Han Solo.

"When you're creating something like (the *Star Wars* saga) the story itself takes over and the characters take over and they begin to tell a story apart from what you're doing," George Lucas explains. "You have to go with it, and it sends you down some very funny paths. Then you have to figure out how to break that apart and put the puzzle back together so it makes sense and

it's cohesive. But that's the adventure
of writing—you're not sure where it's
going to go..."

    Leia, as finally realized, was a
groundbreaking character in her own
right, even if she wasn't the story's
lead. Most fantasy film princesses
were breathtakingly beautiful damsels-
in-distress; that very same year (1977)
produced Jane Seymour as "Princess
Farrah" in Ray Harryhausen's *Sinbad
and the Eye of the Tiger*, a role in the

time-honored tradition of 'scream and faint while you wait for the hero to rescue you'. Although attractive and fresh-faced, Princess Leia was not a centerfold and it's she who rescues the boys from certain doom when they're trapped in the detention area.

Leia aside, there were no significant female characters in either *Star Wars* or *The Empire Strikes Back*, unless you count Aunt Beru or the couple of console-bound Rebels in the hidden base on Hoth. Certainly all of the warriors on display were men, which was logical from a creative standpoint, since the dazzling space dogfights were patterned after their real-life World War II equivalents. Even when these star pilots were being briefed, an effort was made to re-create the classically male look of old war films. (As a point of interest, it was a woman, renowned sci-fi author Leigh Brackett who co-wrote the screenplay for *The Empire Strikes Back*.)

By the time *Return of the Jedi* rolled around, Lucas seemed to realize he needed more of a female sensibility on screen. From one extreme to the other, he a) put Leia in a sexy, pulp-inspired dancing girl outfit and b) made the leader of the Rebel Alliance

a woman, Mon Mothma (Caroline Blakiston). Mon Mothma's part in the movie was brief—she addresses the Rebel Fleet at Frigate Headquarters before their final assault—but she radiates strength, intelligence and compassion, appropriate qualities in a heroic role model, male or female.

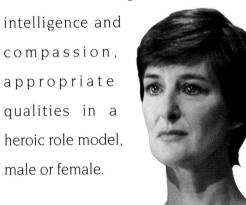

Princess Leia has faced many perils in her quest to liberate the universe, but none so foul as the clammy embrace of her captor, Jabba the Hutt. Below: "The Emperor has made a critical error," announces Mon Mothma as she addresses the Rebel Fleet. "The time for our attack has come." Mon Mothma, portrayed by Caroline Blakiston, was the leader of the Rebel Alliance in Return of the Jedi.

ROMANCE IS AN INTEGRAL INGREDIENT OF THE *Star Wars* TRILOGY. BEFORE LUKE AND LEIA DISCOVERED THEY WERE RELATED, A SPIRITED TRIANGLE INVOLVING HAN SOLO FUELED THE THREE FILMS. HERE, HAN AND LEIA EMBRACE IN A HEARTFELT MOMENT FROM EMPIRE.

"When I saw Star Wars *for the first time, I knew only one thing: I never, ever wanted it to end,"* recalls illustrator REBECCA GUAY. *"To a shy little kid who was mostly a dreamer, and didn't do much of anything else except draw, Star Wars was the best damned thing (Disney World being a close second) that I had ever seen."*

VARIOUS CHARACTERS AND CONCEPTS FOR THE STAR WARS SAGA WERE INTRODUCED IN FICTION APART FROM THE THREE FILMS. THIS IS LUMIYA, A RESOURCEFUL VILLAINESS CREATED FOR THE COMICS.

"Star Wars was supposed to be my first assignment when I went to work for Marvel Comics back in 1986," recalls illustrator COLLEEN DORAN, *"but I missed my chance to draw Lumiya—the female Darth Vader. So, here she is now!"*

PRINCESS LEIA ORGANA—THE "OTHER" YODA ONCE SPOKE ABOUT—IS ALIVE WITH THE FORCE LIKE HER BROTHER AND FATHER. THAT AWESOME ABILITY BRINGS WITH IT AN EQUALLY POWERFUL RESPONSIBILITY.

"I injected a bit of mythology into my depiction of Leia," explains illustrator PAUL LEE. "At some point, clearly, she will become a Jedi Knight. The mask of Vader suggests she is of Vader's blood."

Leia's sensual charms are on display in this figure study. The Princess/freedom-fighter was captured by Jabba the Hutt in *Return of the Jedi* and dressed in an abbreviated costume.

"The challenge here was to be sensual rather then sexist," offers illustrator MIKE GRELL.

The swing across the Death Star chasm; a homage to countless adventure films of the past.

"I like to do portraits and action pictures and experiment with interesting angles of perspective," observes illustrator ZINA SAUNDERS. "I got to combine them all in this portrayal of Luke and Leia on the Death Star."

Leia emerges as a full-fledged Jedi in the final issue of Dark Horse's acclaimed series, Dark Empire. Celebrated comics painter DAVE DORMAN rendered all of the covers, including this one. In addition to the imposing image of Leia, it features Luke in a tense battle with the reborn Emperor.

A scene never seen—a female Rebel searches the icy wastes of Hoth for Han and Luke, perhaps. Women were in short supply in the Rebel ranks, although Mon Mothma was the Alliance leader and Leia was an integral, active character.

"I'm no feminist," declares illustrator LURENE HAINES, "but I think it would have been kind of cool if they actually sent out search parties (in Empire) and some members of the search party would have been women."

POETIC JUSTICE: SLAVE GIRL LEIA LIBERATES HERSELF AND STRANGLES THE LIFE OUT OF HER BLOATED CAPTOR, JABBA THE HUTT, WITH THE CHAIN HE HAD FASTENED TO HER.

"Star Wars was the first 'real' movie I ever saw at the theater," reflects illustrator JILL THOMPSON, "so it's a great feeling to illustrate something that is a part of my childhood memories."

ASTONISHING AS IT SEEMS, THIS EARLY CONCEPT RENDERING OF PRINCESS LEIA DEPICTS HER AS HALF-HUMAN, HALF-MACHINE! ALTHOUGH LUKE WAS SUPPOSED TO BE A FEMALE CHARACTER AT ONE POINT, LEIA WAS ALMOST ALWAYS ENVISIONED AS A FLESH AND BLOOD PRINCESS, MAKING THIS RENDERING SOMETHING OF AN ODDITY.

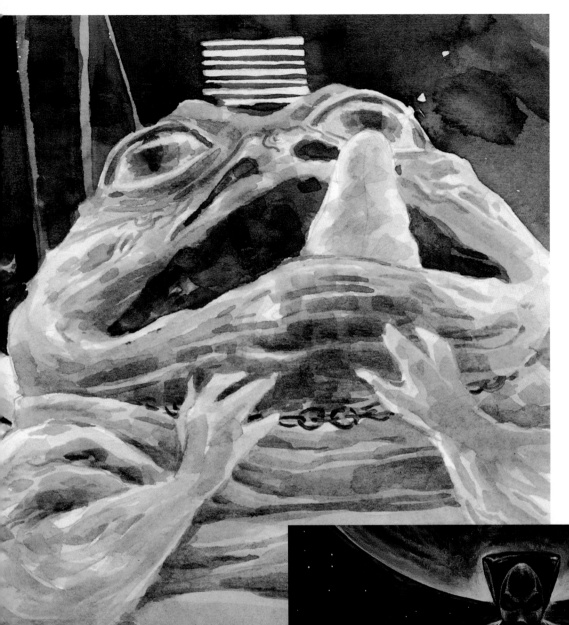

THIS GOUACHE PAINTING FOR THE COVER OF MARVEL COMICS' *STAR WARS #95* WAS RENDERED BY KENT WILLIAMS, A COMICS FAN FAVORITE. IT DEPICTS LUMIYA, THE NEW "DARK LORD"—A CHARACTER CREATED EXPRESSLY FOR THIS MEDIUM.

CHAPTER EIGHT

AN ENIGMA NAMED FETT

Question: How do you top Darth Vader for raw, mythic villainy? Answer: You invent Boba Fett, "the most feared bounty hunter in the galaxy" and certainly the most mysterious. Fett is on screen only briefly during the course of the Saga, yet he has become one of it most enduring characters, perhaps because of the speculative nature of his origin and the simplicity of his purpose and design.

Boba began life as a cartoon character in a short subject called "3241," part of the two-hour CBS *Star Wars Holiday Special* broadcast only once back in November of '78. In that cartoon, produced by Canada's Nelvana Limited, Fett is first presented as a friendly stranger, only to be revealed as an ally of Darth Vader's and a formidable opponent. Although the holiday special was deemed too Hollywoodish by critics and fans alike, the 10-minute animated sequence was widely appreciated. "It was certainly a change of pace for us," remembers Nelvana co-founder Patrick Loubert. "I think it's some of our nicest-looking stuff," his partner, Michael Hirsh, adds. Perhaps someday this unique featurette will be released on home video so all of Fett's followers can again appreciate his debut appearance.

The bounty hunter's costume was

developed by Lucasfilm regulars Ralph McQuarrie and Joe Johnston, working in tandem with Nelvana and Kenner Toys. Initially, Fett's distinctive rig was intended to be worn by "a squad of super-commandos from the Mandalore system", but this idea was quickly abandoned. The flying back-pack, wrist lasers and rocket darts from the original designs were retained and repainted by Johnston, who gave them the appropriate "used" look. Kenner began offering a mail-in premium fig-ure of "Missile-Firing Boba Fett" in the spring of 1979. Due to safety concerns, this version never saw the light of day and consumers got a Boba with the missile glued to his backpack. Later that fall, Kenner unleashed a more dramatic 13½" version of the villain.

All of this led to Boba Fett's first motion picture appearance in *The Empire Strikes Back* (1980). Although Fett (played by Jeremy Bullock) had only a few lines in the film, and wasn't even mentioned by name, he resonated strongly with viewers, as did his equally-memorable spaceship, the *Slave* I, designed by Nilo Rodis-Jamero and inspired by the housings of

unique street lamps near ILM.

No one was surprised when the bounty hunter returned in *Return of the Jedi* a few years later for a lively bout with Han Solo, still partially blinded by his carbon-freezing ordeal. Seeing Fett flying about was a genuine thrill, and many of his gizmos were utilized for the first time. But, alas, his fate was sealed: fighting Han *and* Luke, Boba

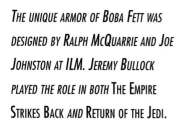

THE UNIQUE ARMOR OF BOBA FETT WAS DESIGNED BY RALPH MCQUARRIE AND JOE JOHNSTON AT ILM. JEREMY BULLOCK PLAYED THE ROLE IN BOTH THE EMPIRE STRIKES BACK AND RETURN OF THE JEDI.

Fett tumbled into the jaws of that insatiable sand monster, the Sarlaac, to what appeared to be a well-deserved demise.

Yet Boba's popularity continued, insuring several additional appearances in various comic books and animated TV programs. Years later, Dark Horse's *Dark Empire* revealed that the Sarlaac simply found Boba's particular brand of armor indigestible, and our favorite bounty hunter was freed to once again terrorize the cosmos.

Of course, many questions regarding Boba Fett's identity and origin remain. Is Fett a Corellian, as some have speculated, or a relative of Han Solo's? What about those Mandolorian super-commandos? And why is the design of his helmet so darn similar to Darth Vader's?

The truth is, these questions are more provocative than any answers Lucas' screenwriters might devise. Boba Fett is a remarkable character *because* he is an enigma, a cool, driven man of action who inspires our imaginations and excites our senses. Long may he remain mysterious!

AS DISTINCTIVE AS ITS CAPTAIN IS BOBA FETT'S SPACESHIP, THE SLAVE I. IT WAS DESIGNED BY NILO RODIS-JAMERO AND INSPIRED BY THE HOUSINGS OF UNIQUE STREET LAMPS NEAR ILM HEADQUARTERS.

BOBA FETT AND THE REPTILIAN BOUNTY HUNTER BOSSKK (FROM *EMPIRE*) ARE SURROUNDED BY ARMED ENEMIES IN THIS IMAGINARY ENCOUNTER. NOTE THAT FETT'S HELMET HAS BEEN BLASTED FROM HIS FACE, REVEALING THIS ARTIST'S INTERPRETATION OF WHAT LIES BENEATH.

Remembers illustrator *DANIEL BRERETON*: "As a kid, I secretly imagined what kind of a guy was Fett...his previous adventures, who he was, and, or course, what was underneath that cool helmet!"

AN AWESOME, PAINTED STUDY OF THE BOUNTY HUNTER IN A TENSE MOMENT FROM *RETURN OF THE JEDI*. ORIGINALLY, BOBA FETT'S ARMORED OUTFIT WAS FAR MORE COLORFUL (BRIGHT BLUES AND REDS). BUT RALPH MCQUARRIE AND JOE JOHNSTON TONED IT DOWN AND EVEN "BEAT IT UP", ADHERING TO GEORGE LUCAS' VISION OF A "USED" UNIVERSE.

"I was always very impressed with Boba Fett," remarks illustrator *JOHN BOLTON*. "He isn't on screen all that much, and he has only a few lines of dialogue. Yet he resonates..."

A UNATTRIBUTED, CARTOON-LIKE RENDER-ING USED TO PROMOTE ONE OF KENNER'S BOBA FETT ACTION FIGURES. SINCE THE BOUNTY HUNTER WAS FEATURED IN BOTH THE FILMS AND THE ANIMATED DROIDS TV SERIES, TWO DIFFERENT FIGURES WERE ULTI-MATELY ISSUED. (FROM THE COLLECTION OF THOMAS H. NEIHEISEL)

A UNIQUE, THREE-DIMENSIONAL RENDER-ING OF OUR FAVORITE HIRED ASSASSIN, COMPLETE WITH THE NASTIEST LOOKING WEAPON IN THE GALAXY.

"*Next to Aunt Beru, Boba Fett has always been my favorite Star Wars character,*" muses illustrator *TOM TAGGART.* "*He always seems to be in complete control of every situation, never losing his cool. And although he doesn't talk much, most people don't realize he has a lovely singing voice. I was thrilled at the chance to illustrate him.*"

JABBA THE HUTT'S PRISON BARGE BECOMES A MAKESHIFT BATTLEFIELD AS LUKE WIPES OUT VARIOUS HENCH-CREATURES WITH HIS LIGHTSABER, MOMENTARILY UNAWARE THAT A FLYING BOBA FETT IS DIRECTLY BEHIND HIM.

"Science fiction and damsels in distress," illustrator *DAVE HOOVER* ponders wistfully. "Exactly my kind of entertainment! The Star Wars films certainly had their share of both..." Color by *JOHN CEBOLLERO*

MORE UNATTRIBUTED PACKAGING ART FROM KENNER: THIS PAINTED PRELIM WAS INTENDED TO PROMOTE A SMALL PLASTIC VERSION OF THE TATOOINE SKIFF FROM *RETURN OF THE JEDI*. KENNER WORKED MINOR MIRACLES IN SIMPLIFYING COMPLEX CHARACTERS AND VEHICLES DEVELOPED BY ILM WITHOUT SACRIFICING AUTHENTICITY. (FROM THE COLLECTION OF THOMAS H. NEIHEISEL)

CHAPTER NINE

ARTIST INDEX

MICHAEL ALLRED

made his comics debut in the early '90s with *Dead Air* (Slave Labor). Other creations include *Graphique Musique*, *The Geek* and *Sandman* from DC and his popular *Madman Adventures* from Dark Horse. NVp.36

KARL ALTSTAETTER

is a writer-artist who got his break a few years back as an assitant at Homage Studios. Since then he has worked for Marvel, DC, Image, and most recently on his own project, *Q-Unit*, for Harris Comics. NVp.89

THOM ANG

is a Project Lead artist for Disney software; he's developed video games for *The Lion King* and other properties. His comics work includes *True Crime #2* for Eclipse (his 1992 debut in the field), a painted card for DC's *Master Series* and a poster for Marvel. NVp.47

SERGIO ARAGONES

began his creative alliance with MAD magazine in 1962. Work for DC followed, including *Bat Lash*, *Plop!*, *Angel and the Ape* and *House of Mystery*. In 1982 he created "Groo the Wanderer." Recent works are *Bell and Buzz* and *Firehouse Five* from Malibu. NVp.96

MARSHALL ARISMAN

is an artist whose paintings and drawings have been widely exhibited both internationally and nationally over the past 20 years. His political cartoons are regularly seen in *The New York Times*, *The Nation*, *Time* and other major publications. NVp.55

DAN BARRY

started in the comics field decades ago with *Flash Gordon* and *Tarzan* newspaper strips. Other early works include *Airboy*, *The Heap* (co-creator), *Valkyrie* and *Daredevil*. *Toyboy*, *Ms. Mystic*, *Predator*, *Crazyman* and *Indiana Jones* represent his more recent accomplishments. NVp.75

JOHN BOLTON

is an award-winning illustrator from England. He's worked on graphic novels and prestige format comics with Chris Claremont, Neil Gaiman, Clive Barker and Anne Rice, among others. Currently, he is rendering *Manbat* for DC. NVp.116

TIM BRADSTREET

began his career as a role playing game artist in 1986, at age 18. He's worked for TSR, FASA and White Wolf, among others. Comics credits include *Hardlooks*, *X*, *Aliens: Music of the Spears*, Clive Barker's *Age of Desire* and *Hawkworld*. NVp.59

DANIEL BRERETON

began his comics career in 1990 with *The Black Terror* mini-series for Eclipse. He followed that award-winning project with *The Psycho* (DC), *Dread* (Eclipse) and numerous comics covers. Recently he illustrated *World's Finest II* (DC). NVp.117

AMANDA CONNER

made her comics debut in the late1980s. Her whimsical style was ideally suited to various Marvel characters (the female Yellowjacket and the wonderful Wasp), assignments for *Archie Comics* and Marvel's new comic based on Disney's *Gargoyles*. NVp77

RON BROWN

graduated from Art Center College of Design (Pasadena, CA) in 1991. He has since been working in feature film animation and as a freelance illustrator. NVp.60

RICARDO DELGADO

wrote and illustrated the dinosaur epic *Age of Reptiles* for Dark Horse and also drew three *Cadillacs and Dinosaurs* covers for Topps Comics. He's also a movie concept artist on projects like *Star Trek: Deep Space Nine* and *True Lies*. NVp.67

FRANK BRUNNER

broke into comics in the early 1970's, rendering *Dr. Strange, Conan, Howard the Duck,* and *Elric* for Marvel Comics. Recently, he illustrated a number of trading cards for Topps (*Jurrasic Park, Mars Attacks* and *Vampirella* among them) and is a chief contributor to the *X-Men* animated TV series. NVp.55

JOE DEVITO

specializes in horror and dinosaur subjects. Recent comics projects include *The Further Adventures of Batman, Superman,* and *Wonder Woman* paperbacks, "Smokin' Lobo" (poster) for DC, a Doc Savage sculpture and cards in *The Creator's Universe.* NVp.95

RICH BUCHLER

has drawn nearly every major character in the DC and Marvel universes. He is the creator of *Deathlok,* the first cyborg in comics, and recently formed New York's Visage Studios with his son Rick. NVp.12

COLLEEN DORAN

has illustrated *Sandman, Amazing Spider-Man, X-Factor* and many others. She is the regular artist for DC's *Valor,* and the creator of *A Distant Soil.* Recent work includes *Legionnaires, Silver Surfer, Guardians of the Galaxy* and *Death Gallery.* NVp.104

GREG CAPULLO

rendered Marvel's *What If?* before beginning his first full-time book, *Quasar,* issues #18-#38. He landed a year-long stay on *X-Force* before departing to Image Comics, where he's completed three "amazingly fun" issues of Todd McFarlane's *Spawn.* NVp.76

NORM DWYER

created and drew Malibu's *Libby Ellis* in 1987 (comics debut), and has worked on numerous titles since then. His most recent project was the ground-breaking computer generated comic book *Donna Matrix* from Reactor's Digital Comics line. NVp.92

BOB FINGERMAN

is a self-confessed sci-fi buff. This interest has manifested itself in comics he's done for *Heavy Metal*, Marvel's *2099 Unlimited*, Dark Horse's *Andrew Vachss' Underground*, and his recent solo title *White Like She* (also Dark Horse). NVp.57

HUGH FLEMING

is an Austrailian illustrator who has painted numerous *Indiana Jones* covers for Dark Horse, the recent *Universal Monsters Illustrated* display box/poster for Topps, and a *Vampirella* trading card, also for Topps. NVp.15

FRANCHESCO

has co-created and illustrated *Adam* for DC's *Green Lantern Corps* and *The Scavengers* for Triumphant. He recently created the visuals to *Schizm* for Marvel's "Barkerverse." NVp.90

DREW FRIEDMAN

has worked on some choice assignments for Topps, the *Barfo* candy containers and *Toxic High School* trading cards among them, in addition to books and various cable TV jobs. NVp.47

RICH GEARY

has been a regular contributor to *National Lampoon*, *Heavy Metal* and *The New York Times Book Review*. His graphic stories have been collected in *At Home With Rick Geary*, *Wonders and Oddities*, *Housebound* and *Prairie Moon*. NVp.64

DAVE GIBBONS

has been working in comics since 1973, drawing *Harlem Heroes*, *Dan Dare*, and *Rogue Trooper* for the British weekly *2000 AD*. Additional work on both sides of the Atlantic includes *Dr. Who*, *Superman*, *Batman*, the Hugo-winning *Watchmen* and *Give Me Liberty*. NVp.63

MIKE GRELL

is an active writer as well as a comics artist. Creations include *Warlock* (DC), *Starslayer* (Pacific/First), *John Sable*, *Freelance* (First), *Shado* (DC) and *Shaman's Tears* (Image). He has rendered *Tarzan* and *Brenda Starr* comic strips. NVp.107

REBECCA GUAY

began her career in comics working on titles such as Marvel *2099 Unlimited*, *Conan* and *Swamp Thing*. Currently, she's penciling *Black Orchid* for DC'S Vertigo line. Her work can also be seen in Paradox's *Big Book of Death*. NVp.105

LURENE HAINES

is recognized for her pencil, color pencil, oil, and watercolor renderings. Noteworthy projects include *Hellraiser*, *Green Arrow: The Longbow Hunters*, *Miss Fury*, *Deep Space Nine* and a book of her own pin-up art, *Femina: Dream Girls*. NVp.109

MATT HALEY

got his start penciling *Star Trek: The Next Generation* (DC) and *Phantom of Fear City* (Claypool), as well as *Brigade* (Image), and the *Ghost* special (Dark Horse). NVp.37

DAVE JOHNSON

CULLY HAMNER

began working with DC back in '91 (*Green Lantern: Mosaic*), then started rendering covers, pin-ups and trading cards for Image and Dark Horse. He currently renders *Firearm* (Malibu's Unltraverse) and is plotting and penciling a feature called "Brave" for Gaijin Studio's *Ground Zero*. NVp.98

RICH HEDDEN

enjoyed his first experience in the professional comic-book biz back in 1986 with Dark Horse's *Roachmill* (he co-created the character). Later work includes mowing lawns, collecting unemployment checks, watching a lot of cable, and mowing more lawns. NVp.54

DAVE HOOVER

began his creative career in animation, working on *Fat Albert*, *Tarzan*, *Flash Gordon*, *Fire and Ice* and *Starchaser: The Legend of Orin*. In the late '80s he switched to comics, starting at DC, then moving on to Marvel (he presently renders *Captain America*). NVp.119

JANINE JOHNSTON

made her comics debut with Dark Horse's *Tales of the Jedi*. *Elfquest: Blood of Ten Chiefs* followed, and she is now the regular cover artist for that series and *Poison Elves*, from Mulehide Graphics. NVp.58

JEFFREY JONES

has been both a comics professional and book cover artist since 1967. He's worked for Warren, DC, Last Gasp, Pacific, King, Gold Key, *National Lampoon* ("Idyl") and *Heavy Metal* ("I'm Age"). NVp.127

KELLEY JONES

has been dazzling fans for a number of years with his sophisticated linework. In the '80s he rendered a pair of *Deadman* series for DC and more recently he's illustrated *Dark Joker* (also for DC) and the five-part *Aliens: Hive* for Dark Horse. NVp.41

MIRAN KIM

is an accomplished record cover artist (*Death Metal* for Relapse Records) and paperback illustrator (horror covers for Dell-Abyss). Comics-related work includes *Hellraiser* (1991-93) and trading card paintings for Topps, including *Mars Attacks*. NVp.40

JACK KIRBY

was the undisputed King of Comics. In the business since the late '30s (starting with *Jumbo Comics*), he and Stan Lee transformed Marvel into a fantasy powerhouse in the '60s with creations such as *The Fantastic Four*, *X-Men*, *The Incredible Hulk* and a new incarnation of *Captain America*, among many others. NVp.38

RAY LAGO

was an award-winning commercial illustrator before he switched to comics, starting with Marvel's *Open Space* series. Other covers include *Ivanhoe* (First), Marvel/Epic's *Hellraiser* and various Dark Horse titles, *Predator: Cold War* and *Robocop: Mortal Coils* among them. NVp.45

ZOHAR LAZAR

studied art in New York City and made his professional illustration debut with his *Star Wars Galaxy 2* rendering. He is influenced by fine art and modern sculpture, as well as the graphic novels of Bill Sienkiewicz and other painters working in the comics field. NVp.99

JAE LEE

is a celebrated illustrator whose past works include *Marvel Comics Presents*, *Uncanny X-Men*, *X-Factor* and *Namor* for Marvel; *Youngblood: Strikefile* and *WildC.A.T.S. Trilogy* for Image. His own creation, *Hellshock*, is also from Image. NVp.62

MIKE MAYHEW

has penciled the *Praxis* series in *Justice League Quarterly* for DC Comics. Currently his life revolves around the new *Zorro* comic book series published by Topps. NVp.90

PAUL LEE

is a graduate of the Art Center College of Design. He worked on the now infamous *True Crimes* trading card sets. His paintings have been featured in *Playboy*, *Omni*, *L.A. Weekly* and can also be seen at the Sarah Bain Gallery in Brea, California. NVp.106

WALTER McDANIEL

trained with the likes of Gil Ashbey, Michael Davis, Rich Buckler and Neal Adams. He currently works for Marvel Comics, Milestone and Image Comics. NVp.37

JOHN PAUL LONA

got his professional start illustrating in the gaming industry for West End Games' *Star Wars* line. He has since done work for other gaming companies, including GDW, TSR and FASA. NVp.58

MIKE McMAHON

is an illustrator who is adept at both realism and abstractionism. In 1976, he did his first professional comics work; later that year he started drawing *Judge Dredd* for IPC magazines. NVp.93

DAVID LOWERY

began his film illustration career at George Lucas' famed ILM, storyboarding *Willow*. Recent films include *Jurassic Park*, *Bram Stoker's Dracula*, *Hook*, *The Flintstones* and *The Rocketeer*. NVp.68

LINDA MEDLEY

is a comics professional whose work has appeared in DC's *Action Comics*, *Justice League*, *Wonder Woman* and *Who's Who*, as well as *The Galactic Girl Guards* (Tundra). She recently penciled *The Doom Patrol* for Vertigo. NVp.64

SHAWN C. MARTINBROUGH

studied at the Children's Art carnival in Harlem, then went on to illustrate a short story in Clive Barker's *Hellraiser* series along with several renderings for Marvel Comics' Epic division. NVp.97

DAVID O. MILLER

works in a New York studio and has contributed to *Dungeons and Dragons* magazine, *Spelljammer*, *Buck Rogers* and *Dark Sun* for TSR, *ARS Magica* and *Vampire* for White Wolf and *Mythius* for GDW. NVp.65

C. SCOTT MORSE

co-created, illustrated, and self-published the comic book series *Ancient Siege*. Current comics work includes a creator-owned limited series, *Soulwind*. NVp.76

NELSON

broke into comics with a fully-painted cover for *Ghost Rider #18* (Marvel). Other work includes *Robocop* projects for Dark Horse, a *Jurassic Park* painted card for Topps and his own creation, *The Eudaemon*, for Dark Horse/Manta Comics. NVp.46

HOANG NGUYEN

made his comics debut with *Robocop 3* (Dark Horse). Since then he's worked for both Marvel (*Alien Legion*) and DC (the Impact line). More recent work includes the *Punisher War Zone* project and *Judge Dredd* for DC. NVp.48

KEVIN O'NEILL

co-created London's famed *2000 A.D. Weekly* back in 1976. Freelance credits include *Ro-Busters*, *Green Lantern Corps*, *Metalzoic*, *Marshall Law*, *Legend of the Dark Knight*, *Lobo Convention Special* and *Pinhead vs. Marshall Law*. NVp.94

MARK PACELLA

provided illustrations for *The New York Times Book Review* before turning to comics. At Marvel, he worked on their various *X-Men* titles. Now at Rob Liefeld's Extreme Studios, he's recently developed a new book entitled *Dooms IV*. NVp.67

JIMMY PALMIOTTI

is an inker who began in the comics field with Malibu Comics' *Ex-Mutant*s and Marvel's *The Nam*. More recent accomplishments include *The Punisher*, *Judge Dredd*, *X*, *Xombie*, *Solar* and *Ninjak*. His penciling abilities are displayed in Malibu's *Genesis #0*. NVp.43

JASON PEARSON

began his comics career in 1990 with a *Legion of Super-Heroes* job at DC. This was followed by *The Uncanny X-Men* (Marvel) and the recent *Savage Dragon* mini-series for Image Comics. NVp.80

BRANDON PETERSON

is an accomplished comics art illustrator who has worked on Marvel's *X-Men* titles and is currently drawing *Codename: Stryke-Force* for Image. NVp.44

JOE PHILLIPS

has drawn over fifty comic book issues since the mid-'80s. Titles include *Speed Racer*, *Mister Miracle*, *Timberwolf*, *Silver Surfer*, *The Incredible Hulk* and his new series, *Quantum 5*. NVp.83

WHILCE PORTACIO

got his big break in comics inking *Longshot*, *Alien Legion* and *Alpha Flight*. Penciling gigs on *Punisher*, *X-Factor* and *Uncanny X-Men* followed. Recent projects include *Wetworks* (Image) and ten Dracula renderings for Topps' *Universal Monsters Illustrated* cards. NVp.69

RALPH REESE

is a comics/fantasy artist who's been successfully avoiding superheroes for the past twenty years. Projects include *National Lampoon* gigs, children's books and inking for Valiant's *Magnus, Robot Fighter* comic. NVp.79

SYLVAIN

was born in France and trained under Neal Adams in the early '80s. He recently completed *Fountain of Youth* written by his mentor, Moebius, and his color work has appeared in Topps' *Cadillacs and Dinosaurs*. NVp.42

ZINA SAUNDERS

has been producing illustrations for advertising, theater posters, books and videocassette covers, including a couple of Godzilla classics. She is also an active trading card artist for DC and Topps (her dad, famed painter Norm Saunders, rendered the original *Mars Attacks*). NVp.107

TOM TAGGART

rendered unique "3D" covers for *Batman, Swamp Thing, Doom Patrol* and *Animal Man* (all DC). He's also done creative work for *Elfquest, Zen* and *Silver Skull*. NVp.118

CHRIS SPROUSE

made his professional comics debut with DC's *Hammerlocke*. Since then he's worked on various DC and Marvel titles, including *Batman, Justice League, X-Men, Legion of Super-Heroes* and its spinoff, *Legionnaires*. NVp.88

JILL THOMPSON

has illustrated comics for various publishers, including *Sandman, Wonder Woman*, the new *Black Orchid* (all DC) and *The Scarlet Letter* for *Classics Illustrated*. She recently completed *The Badger* for Dark Horse. NVp.110

JIM STARLIN

started working in comics in 1971; credits include *Captain Marvel, Warlock, Superman, Batman, Dreadstar, Breed* (a trilogy mini-series for Bravura) and a pair of novels with Diana Graziunas: *Among Madmen* and *Lady El*. NVp.91

TIM TRUMAN

broke into comics with back-up stories for *Sgt. Rock* in 1980. Credits include *Grimjack, Time Beavers, Airboy, The Prowler* (his own retro-pulp concept), *Jonah Hex, Turok*, an updated Hawkman for DC's *Hawkworld* and *The Lone Ranger* for Topps. NVp.61

ARTHUR SUYDAM

began his comics career in 1973 with DC's *House of Secrets*. Work for *Heavy Metal* and *Epic Illustrated* followed. His creations include *Mugwog*, the popular *Cholly and Flytrap*, along with various book jacket and movie poster assignments. NVp.41

KEITH TUCKER

combines comics work with film and TV-related assignments. Work includes *Tom and Jerry, Garfield, Animaniacs, Duck Tales* and *Conan* (storyboards), *Star Trek II* and *The Thing* (live-action FX) and *Tiny Toons* and *The Little Mermaid* (painting and penciling). NVp.89

JEFF WATTS

attended the Calabasis Art Institute in L.A., then entered the film industry, finding this a very fertile area in which to perfect his drafting and painting skills. His influences range in diversity from Frazetta to Frans Hals and Dean Cornwall. NVp.96

MIKE ZECK

began drawing comics professionally in 1975 with Charlton assignments, moving on to Marvel with *Master of Kung-Fu*, *Capatin America*, *Secret Wars*, *Spider-Man* and *The Punisher*. He currently plans a *Batman* story for DC later this year. NVp.56

BORIS VALLEJO

was born in Lima, Peru. In addition to movie posters and books, his celebrated paintings have appeared on everything from drinking glasses to jigsaw puzzles. Twelve volumes of his collected works have been published all over the world. *Box Art* p.87, cover.

AN ARTFUL STUDY OF ONE OF EMPEROR PALPATINE'S IMPERIAL GUARDS BY THOM ANG. IT WAS USED IN THE DEVELOPMENT OF ANG'S NEW VISION PAINTING, FEATURED ON PAGE 47.

THERE'S NO PLACE LIKE HOME, EVEN IF IT IS A CLAMMY LITTLE HUT NESTLED IN THE SWAMPLANDS OF DAGOBAH. YODA'S RESIDENCE AND SURROUNDING ENVIROMENT, AS RENDERED BY JEFFREY JONES.

SNEAK PREVIEW

THIS THRILLING AERIAL VIEW OF THE AT-AT BATTLE ON HOTH WAS ILLUSTRATED BY **STEVE REISS**. IT IS ONE OF MANY PREVIOUSLY UNPUBLISHED ARTWORKS SOON TO BE EXHIBITED IN *STAR WARS GALAXY THREE*.